B
ne.. ...
Motorways

or

A Break from the Motorways

By

HUGH CANTLIE

Co-author of

5 minutes off the motorway

(1995)

Over 200 pubs, hotels, restaurants and places of interest which are about five minutes from a motorway junction.

———

Published by Cheviot Books

1st Edition Sep 2001   Reprint Jan 2002
2003 Edition Sep 2002
2004 Edition Oct 2003

Copyright	© Hugh Cantlie
Illustrations	© Hugh Cantlie
Plans	© Paul Cantlie
Maps	© John Lee
Front Cover	© Tracy Coxon

Cheviot Books,
Belford Hall, Belford, Northumberland NE70 7EY
Website: www.cheviotbooks.com
Email: enquiries@cheviotbooks.co.uk
Tel: 01668 213 313 FAX: 01668 213 778

ISBN 0-9539920-2-0

Printed and bound by SGC Printing,
Merthyr Tydfil, CF48 3TD

The Motorway Network

ACKNOWLEDGEMENTS

I would like to thank Cadogan Guides for their permission to reuse some of the original illustrations which appeared in "5 Minutes Off the Motorway" first printed in 1995 and for relinquishing their rights to this publication.

My gratitude is due to the many others without whose help this guide could not have been produced. My thanks especially to my brother Paul for our joint efforts in producing 5 Minutes off the Motorway and for redrawing the junction plans for Breaks near the Motorways. To Tracy Coxon, who had to transfer old fashioned typing and drawings to modern methods of printing, designing the front cover and then teaching me how to use a laptop. To John Lee for his work in producing the maps of each motorway and to Mary Murray for helping with the update. Max Herford for his advice on the front cover and Ned Hoste for design of the layout. Thanks also are due to Jon Bessant and his colleagues at Stephens & George Limited for their technical assistance before printing.

My thanks are due to all the help I have received from the publishing and book trade such as to those at Cheviot Books especially Daisy Leyland in sorting out deliveries, queries and keeping in touch with the patient people at Gardners and Bertrams and to Rita Cremona at Book Data.

Last but not least I am grateful to all those readers who wrote in to suggest places which might be included or or excluded. This made it much easier for me to check them out for myself before coming to a decision. The names of those people who have contributed to this edition with the places which have been accepted are given separately. Please continue the good work!

Contents

Introduction

The Purpose of the Guide

Nearly every motorway junction seems to offer the possibility of getting away from the pressure of intensive driving for a short while for a meal or a break in calmer surroundings. It is only the uncertainty of whether such a haven exists or how long it will take to resume the journey that makes you reluctant to risk leaving the motorway. This guide seeks to remove that uncertainty.

Assessment

This is not a list of gastronomic feasts but of places which have a friendly and cheerful ambiance.

Our assessments were based on unannounced and anonymous visits, so the opinions expressed are free of any considerations other than what we considered to be places with a congenial atmosphere.

Particular mention is made of landlords' attitudes to children and dogs as many of the users will be travelling with their families.

For those of us who have to make more frequent stops, some places have been included which should be treated more as "comfort stops" but nevertheless are more cheerful than a motorway service station.

Pubs of some well known chains have been omitted because we did not feel that they were markedly different from those we were trying to avoid. It is a sad reflection that so many places are now owned by national or international groups who impose the same style of decoration, food and furniture throughout their outlets with little regard for local styles.

Some motorways had no places worth visiting so have not been included.

Motorway Maps and Plans

The layout is relatively easy to follow. The motorways are in numerical order with a separate section for Scotland. Each map is orientated with north at the top. The scale depends on what has to be shown and how to fit it on to the page. The longer motorways have been divided up into sections.

Those junctions with places off them are shown with the appropriate junction number, whilst those with nothing to get off for are blank. This helps you work out the distances involved between likely stops.

Junction Plans

There is a short introduction of any difficulties you may find (from personal experience) together with a plan. Filling stations are shown thus 🛢. Entries are shown by a letter i.e. Ⓐ which corresponds with their write up below. Places of interest nearby are shown.

Places of Interest

The names of historic houses or places of interest nearby are given with the initials in brackets of the owners where known. Those houses owned by members of the Historic Houses Association need to be contacted beforehand.

(EH)	*English Heritage.*
(HHA)	*Historic Houses Association.*
(HS)	*Historic Scotland.*
(NT)	*National Trust.*
(NTS)	*National Trust for Scotland.*

Entries

A brief description is given of each entry, to include attitudes to dogs and children and the times for the last orders for food as opposed to drinks. The number of bedrooms where applicable, and which are shown as 🛏
The price range is shown by the number of £s
The drawing gives an idea of what the place looks like to help recognition upon arrival. Those places with particular character are shown with an ✳

Prices

We have tried to give an indication of the price range based on an 8oz sirloin steak as a marker. These are as follows:

Under £8	£
£8-£10	££
£10-15	£££
Over £15	££££

The first two categories could be classified as good Pub food.
The bedroom prices seeem to equate with that of the food.

Readers Response

Our findings were subjective at the time but you may well find that places have become less good or have improved. If so please write to us, using the listing sheets at the back and receive not only our thanks and a free copy of the guide but also the gratitude of other motorists.

Readers Contributions

Additions

A1(M)
44	Chequers	Tim O'Connor-Fenton
48	Rose Manor Hotel	David Northam,
49	Nags Head	Tim O'Connor-Fenton

M1
14	Carrington Arms	Mrs J.C Emmott

M4
17	Neeld Arms	Vana Barlow
18	Hinton Grange Hotel	P. Egerton-Warburton
27	Rising Sun	Grace Packer

M6
43	Killoran Hotel	Francis Taylor

M11
11	Queens Head	Tim O'Connor-Fenton
12	The Orchard	Fiddes Payne

M54
4	Hundred House Hotel	Jimmie Ferard

Deletions

A1(M)
48	White Swan	Francis Gradidge

M5
14	The Huntsman	Tim O'Connor-Fenton

M48
2	The Bridge Inn	Tim Horn

A1(M)

London to Newcastle

6 to **63**

The A1 was the old Great North Road between London and Edinburgh. The building of the M1 and the M6 reduced its importance but with the level of traffic rising efforts were and are being made to upgrade it to motorway standard. At the moment only six sections have been so modernised but the numbering of the junctions is on the basis that they will all be linked up eventually. These sections are; the southern part from the M25 to Baldock, the Peterborough section, the Doncaster section, the junction with the M1, the Boroughbridge part and lastly the section from Scotch Corner to Newcastle.

SOUTHERN SECTION **6** to **10**

A boring stretch getting out of London.

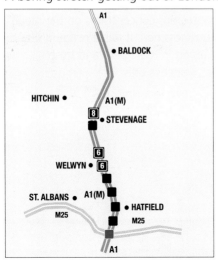

6 Welwyn Garden City A1000

A complicated system of roundabouts, but worth the effort as Welwyn (as opposed to Welwyn Garden City) is a pleasant market town to this day.

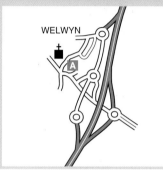

WELWYN

Places of interest
The Roman Baths.
George Bernard
Shaw's house at
Ayton
St Lawrence.

Ⓐ The White Hart

Welwyn
☎ 01438 715 353
Last orders: 2.00pm. Closed on Sundays.
££

Once a Georgian coaching inn, it no longer has bedrooms but concentrates on bar meals for local businessmen. It has a restaurant and bar specialising in roast beef and fresh vegetables. Lunches only.

8   Hitchin
Stevenage (N) A602

Stevenage was once a sleepy country town
and then became one of the first New Towns
in the 1950s. There is little reason to go
through it, unless to visit Knebworth House,
for which Junction 7 is closest. The village of

Little Wymondley is
attractive in rather
a chintzy way but
nevertheless
pleasant. Graveley
on the Old Great
North Road has
changed little.

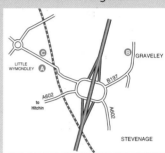

The Bucks Head

Little Wymondley
☎ 01438 353 320
Last orders: 2.15pm and 9.30pm
9.00pm on Sundays.
£

It has been an inn since it was built some 400
years ago. It is a locals' pub without frills but
with a children's playground, a family room,
outside seating, a car park and
Petanque. Children and
dogs are welcome.
A comfort stop.

| 8 | Hitchin
Stevenage (N) A602 |

Ⓑ The Wagon and Horses

Graveley

☎ 01438 367 658

Last orders: 2.30pm and 9.00pm,
No evening meals on Sundays.

ff

It was most probably a coaching
stop but is now a
country pub/restaurant.
It has a beer garden
overlooking the
village pond.
A comfort stop.

Ⓒ Plume of Feathers

Little Wymondley

☎ 01438 729 503

Last orders: 2.00pm and 9.15pm.
No evening meals on Sundays

ff

A small 18th Century house which has been
made into a pub. With a restaurant and a bar,
a children's playground
and outside seating .
Children and dogs
are welcome.

PETERBOROUGH SECTION

13 to 17

The most recent part of the A1(M) to be built to motorway standards. It is unusual in having four lanes which could be a sign of future growth in traffic.

Not the most attractive part of England but Huntingdon is redolent of Cromwell and there are some interesting places, such as Buckden Palace and Island Hall. The area seems to be full of disused airfields from World War II, when British and American bomber bases were sited all over this part of the country.

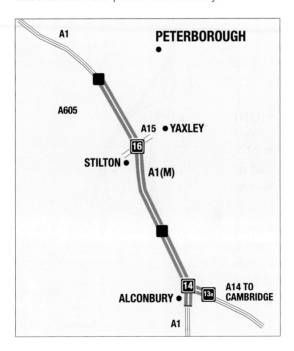

13/14 Alconbury Huntingdon A14

A difficult junction but it is a way for those, driving down from the north to switch over to the A14 to go to Cambridge. For those trying to regain the road going north, you have to go through the same procedure, but head north on the A14 which then rejoins the A1.

Places of interest
Ramsey Abbey Gatehouse (NT)
Monks Wood Nature Reserve.

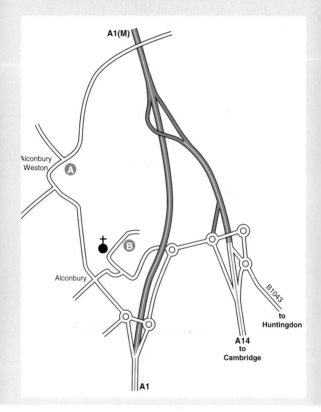

13/14 Alconbury
Huntingdon A14

Ⓐ The White Hart
Alconbury Weston
☎ 01480 890 331
Last orders: 2.00pm and 9.00pm.
9.30pm on Fridays and Saturdays.
No evening meals on Sundays.
££

A pleasant rural village pub. No particular
facilities except a dart board but a friendly
atmosphere and hearty bar meals. Large
beer gardern with
rabbits and guinea
pigs to amuse
children.
Dogs outdoors
but controlled.

Ⓑ The Manor House Hotel
Alconbury
☎ 01480 890 423
Last orders:
2.00pm and 9.00pm. No evening meals
on Sundays.
££

A 17th Century house now a privately
owned pub/ hotel. It has a restaurant and
bar with a garden at the rear.
There are 4 double
bedrooms.
No children
or dogs.

16 Peterborough A15

The junction is easy, but finding one's way through Yaxley is more difficult. Head for the steeple of the church as a landmark and then left at the T junction beyond. The Three Horseshoes is along the village street on the right. No difficulty to find the Bell Inn in Stilton.

Places of interest
Peterborough Cathedral.
Elton Hall (HHA).
Southwick Hall (HHA)

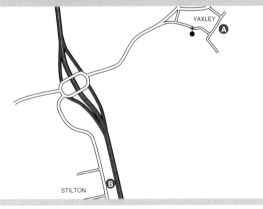

A Three Horseshoes
Yaxley
☎ 01733 242 059
Last orders: 2.00pm and 9.00pm.
9.30pm on Fridays and Saturdays.
££

A cosy pub on the main street of the village which serves bar meals. A children's playground, beer garden and a car park at the rear.

16 | Peterborough A15

B Bell Inn Hotel

Stilton

☎ 01733 241 066

Last orders: 2.00pm and 9.30pm.
2.00pm and 9.30pm Sundays.

£££ 🛏 ✶

A 16th century coaching inn and now a
privately owned well furnished hotel with
19 bedrooms, two bars and a restaurant
on two levels under beamed ceilings. There
is outside seating in an enclosed garden
and private parking. Dick Turpin's room
where he rested between operations is still
in use as the resident's lounge. Those
looking for Stilton cheese will be
disappointed as it was made in Melton
Mowbray and sold here on the old
coaching route. The place is haunted so
dogs are not welcome.

DONCASTER SECTION

34 to **38**

One of the original sections to be rebuilt as a motorway. It is also intersects with the M18 linking the M1 to the M62.

At the southern end it starts north of Blyth at a roundabout with the A614. After the junction with the M18 it passes to the west of Doncaster and ceases as a motorway at Junction 38.

Just after it reverts to being a dual carriageway on the right of the road going north, there is a strange small building in fine ashlar stone. This is Robin Hood's Well which was designed by Sir John Vanbrugh for the 3rd Earl of Carlisle.

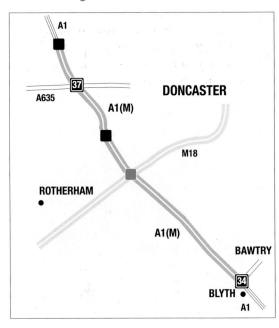

34	Bawtry A614 Worksop B6045

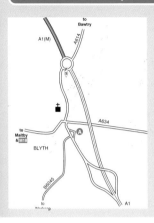

An easy junction but for those driving up from the south, it is best to get off onto the slip road a mile or so beforehand which is signed Maltby A634.

Ⓐ

White Swan

Blyth
☎ 01909 591 222
Last orders: 2.00pm and 9.30pm.
No meals on Sunday evenings.
££

A small pub overlooking the village green with some outside seating. It serves bar meals especially fish and the rest is home made. Due to the resident hounds dogs are discouraged as well as children, as it is too small to cope.

37 Barnsley
Doncaster A635

A straightforward junction posing no problems. A filling station just beyond Marr Lodge.

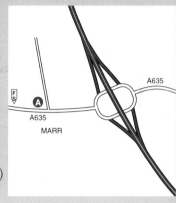

Places of interest
Brodsworth Hall (EH)
Cusworth Hall

Ⓐ Marr Lodge

Marr
☎ 01302 390 355
Last orders: 11.00pm. 10.30pm on Sundays.
££

A modern building, but it caters for the passing motorist, especially those on their way to or from Brodsworth Hall. It serves bar type meals in various open plan bars. Most of the food is home made. No dogs but children welcome.

London to Newcastle

BOROUGHBRIDGE SECTION

44 to **49**

This section is in two parts, both of recent construction. The short southern section is the junction with the recently completed M1 extension. From Junction 45 it is a dual carriageway until Junction 46, skirting past Wetherby which northerners consider to be the gateway to their home stretch. At Junction 49 a decision has to be taken whether to continue on the A1 to Scotch Corner or head for Newcastle on the A19 past Middlesborough.

Boroughbridge is a pleasant market town.

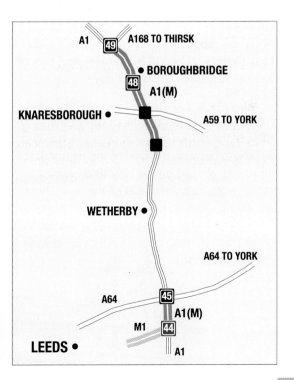

44 Ledsham

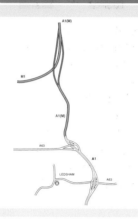

Ledsham is 3 miles south of the M1 and A1(M) interchange. It is surprisingly easy to find as there are feeder roads coming off the A1(M) in both directions

Places of interest
Huddlestone Hall

 # Chequers Inn
Ledsham
☎ 01977 683 135
Last Orders 2.15 and 9.15pm. From 11am on Saturdays. Closed all day Sunday
£££ *

A Free House in the middle of this Estate village. The reason why it is closed all day on Sunday is because the lady of the manor in 1830 was abused on her way to church by estate workers pouring out of the pub. There are eating areas downstairs and a comfortable restaurant upstairs. The two chefs cook to order from an imaginative menu. Well behaved children and dogs are welcome.

45 Leeds
Tadcaster A64

For those going to Bramham on the dual carriageway, come off the A1 at the next exit as they would with a motorway.

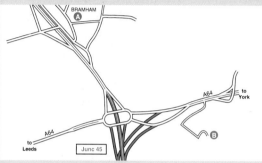

Places of interest
Bramham Park. (HHA)

Ⓐ **The Red Lion**
Bramham
☎ 01937 843 524
Last orders: 2.00pm and 8.45pm.
No evening meals on Sunday.
££

A typical village pub, which has been extended by annexing the butcher's shop next door as a restaurant. A cheerful place with attentive service. A beer garden and car park. Children and dogs welcome. A comfort stop.

45 Leeds
Tadcaster A64

Hazelwood Castle Hotel

Hazelwood

☎ 01937 535 353

Last orders: 9.45pm in the restaurant (which does not serve lunches except on Sundays) From 11.00am to 9.30pm in the Bistro.

££££

An imposing pile set in 77 acres of grounds. Listed in the Domesday Book it was crenellated in 1290. It has now been converted into a privately owned hotel with 21 bedrooms. Previously it was occupied by Carmelite monks, who would have had a simpler life style than that now offered. These include the 1086 Restaurant, a cookery school, conference and banqueting suites, musical events and clay pigeon shoots. For those in more of a rush there is the Prickly Pear Bistro, as well as breakfasts.

48 Knaresborough A6055
Boroughbridge A168

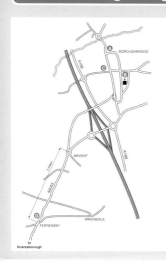

A dumbbell form with roundabouts at each end. Boroughbridge was a coaching stop on the Great North Road.

Places of interest
Roman town of Isurium.

The Crown
Boroughbridge
☎ 01423 322 328
Last orders: 9.30pm. No lunches in the restaurant except on Saturdays. Breakfast.
£££ Breakfast

An old coaching inn since 1672, it has now been fully modernised to have 37 bedrooms, a swimming pool, sauna and gym.
A comfortable restaurant and bars.
No dogs.
Breakfasts.

48 Knaresborough A6055
Boroughbridge A168

B

The Dining Room
Boroughbridge
☎ 01423 326 426
Last orders: 2.00pm and 9.00pm
No evening meals on Sundays.
£££

A family owned restaurant in the centre of
the town, which was opened some two years
ago. It is small and comfortable
with an imaginative
menu. Well behaved
children and dogs
allowed.
Advisable to
reserve.

C

Rose Manor Hotel
Boroughbridge
☎ 01423 322 245
Last orders: 2.00pm and 9.00pm.
9pm on Sundays.
£££ 🛏

A privately owned hotel in its
own grounds with 20
bedrooms and a restaurant
It is well known for
its excellent afternoon
teas. Children
welcome.

General Tarleton

Ferrensby
☎ 01423 340 284
Last orders: 2.15pm and 9.30pm
8.30pm on Sundays.
£££ 🛏 ✳

A privately owned restaurant and hotel with 14
bedrooms. It is reputed to have the best
cuisine in Yorkshire with a warm welcome from
a young professional staff in a relaxed
atmosphere. Dogs and children welcome
provided they behave.

49 Thirsk A168 Ripon

You can get off the A168 and return to the A1 easily enough, provided you follow the plan.

The Nags Head is some 8 miles north of Junction 49 so only just within reach. There is a turning to the east off a gap in the carriageway to Pickhill.

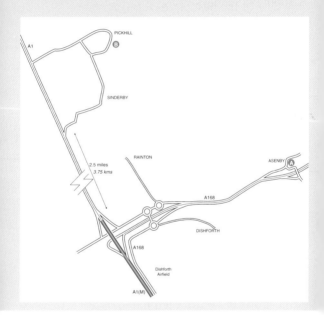

49	Thirsk A168
	Ripon

Ⓐ The Crab and Lobster
Asenby
☎ 01845 577 286
Last orders: 2.15pm and 9.15 pm
2.00pm and 9.00 pm on Sundays.
££££ 🛏 ✱

One of the best places for a stopover on a
motorway! The decor has been done with
flair and the set menu (which obviously
specialises in fish) is value for money.
The Crab Manor Hotel next door
is in the same ownership
and has 11 bedrooms
with an eclectic mix
of furniture and styles.

Ⓑ Nags Head
Pickhill
☎ 01845 567 391
Last orders: 2.00pm and 9.30 pm
£££ 🛏 Breakfast ✱

It is really a restaurant in an agricultural
village with a seperate dining room and a
well appointed bar. A good wine list and
much frequented by the surrounding folk.
There are 16 bedrooms.
Children and
dogs allowed.

NEWCASTLE SECTION

56 to 63

The most northerly section built to motorway standards so far. It starts at Scotch Corner and ends south of Gateshead with a spur leading towards the Tyne Tunnel. At Scotch Corner in coaching and early motoring days, a decision had to made whether to head for Scotland via the old Roman road to Penrith in Cumberland or else to continue up the east coast to Edinburgh.

This stretch is not very interesting but Durham Cathedral "the loveliest building on Planet Earth" is just off the motorway and the Angel of the North will greet you at the other end.

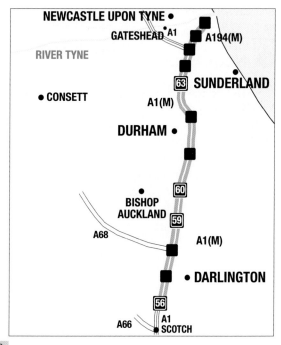

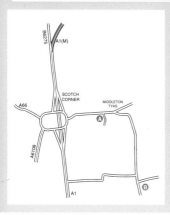

There are no places near this junction, but two miles to the south is the junction with the A66 known as Scotch Corner, where there are two excellent places.

The Shoulder of Mutton

Middleton Tyas
☎ 01325 377 271
Last orders: 2.00pm and 10.00pm.
£££ ＊

A picturesque and friendly country pub in the village. It has a restaurant upstairs and a beamed ceiling bar where traditional hot and cold food is served. No dogs.

The Black Bull

Moulton
☎ 01325 377 289
Last orders: 2.00pm and 10.00pm.
Closed Sundays.
££££ *

One of the best known places in this part of Yorkshire and privately owned. It has a conservatory restaurant as well as several dining areas and a bar which serves bar meals. In addition there is Hazel - a Pullman carriage from the Brighton Belle- which is used for dinners. No children under 7. It is advisable to book.

London to Newcastle

59 Darlington
Newton Aycliffe A167

The Foreseters Arms is on the left at the end
of the stretch of dual carriageway.

To get to The County, skirt past the
roundabout and just beyond the church turn
right at the traffic lights. Ignore the pub
which is on the bend facing you but turn right
again onto the village green. The County is
immediately to the left.

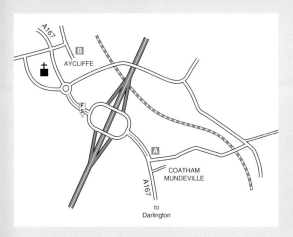

59 Darlington
Newton Aycliffe A167

Ⓐ Foresters Arms
Coatham Mundeville
☎ 01325 320 565
Last Orders 3.00pm and 9.45pm.
Closed Sunday evenings.
£

A typical country pub but with a small restaurant and bars. Outside there is a children's playground and seating when the sun shines.
Dogs are however not welcomed.
A comfort stop.

Ⓑ The County
Aycliffe Village
☎ 01325 312 273
Last Orders 2.00pm and 9.30pm
No evening meals on Sundays.
£££

A country style pub on the village green.
Its was brought to public notice as Tony Blair brought President Chirac of France to have dinner here.
Restricted outside seating.
Children suffered
but no dogs.
French not
essential.

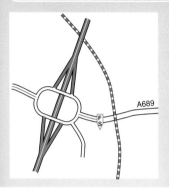

The hotel is
signed from the
junction.

Places of interest
Bishop Auckland
Palace.
Sedgefield
Racecourse.

Hardwick Hall Hotel
Sedgefield
☎ 01740 620 253
Last Orders 2.00pm and 9.30pm either in the
restaurant or in the Bistro.
££££

Once an 18th Century mansion, it still stands in
its original grounds of 120 acres designed by
James Paine which are now listed Grade II*. It
has been enlarged and extended into a modern
hotel and conference centre with 50 bedrooms
where visitors continue to be well cared for.
There is a restaurant and a bar called the Inn
on the Park. A golf course is next door.
Children but no dogs.

63 Chester Le Street

An easy junction to start with as Lumley Castle is signed. Then the signs disappear but keep bearing left and they will reappear.

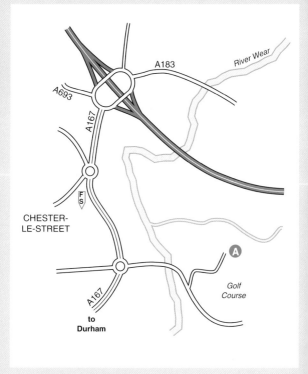

Places of interest

St Peter's Church in Chester le Street (where St Cuthbert's body rested for a 100 years before final burial at Durham Cathedral).
Beamish Open Air Museum.

63 Chester Le Street

 A

Lumley Castle
Chester Le Street
☎ 0191 389 1111
Last orders: 2.00pm and 9.30pm.
No lunches on Saturdays.
££££   🛏   ✶

Built in 1389 by Sir Ralph Lumley it is still
owned by the family. For the past 25 years it
has been leased out as a friendly, efficient and
comfortable hotel with 59 bedrooms. The
Great Hall is still used for its original purpose to
welcome guests for a meal but there are two
other excellent restaurants and a bar serving
sandwiches. It is surrounded by 9 acres of
garden and over the road there is a golf
course. Although the bedrooms are all
plumbed, the roof structures and massive walls
prevent the installation of lifts. Children but no
dogs

NEWCASTLE
UPON-TYNE

CARLISLE

M6

A1(M)

LEEDS
M55 M65   M1   •YORK
        M62   M62 •HULL
        M61 M6   M181
M57 M58   MANCHESTER M18 M180
LIVERPOOL M6   M6   A1(M)
M63 M56   SHEFFIELD
        M6
CHESTER
SHREWSBURY •M54   M1   •PETERBOROUGH
        M6 M6 TOLL
        M42   A1(M)
BIRMINGHAM M69
        M6
M42   COVENTRY   •CAMBRIDGE
        M45   M11
M50   M40   A1(M)
        M5   M1   M25
M48   M4   LONDON
SWANSEA• M4   M2
CARDIFF   M4   M25 M26 M20
BRISTOL   M3   M23   •FOLKE
M5   M27 A3(M)
        SOUTHAMPTON
•EXETER

A3(M)

Horndean to Portsmouth

1 to **5**

A short stretch of motorway, completed in 1979, to ease the junction of the A3 to the M27.

Coming from the north after Petersfield it passes Butser Ancient Farm before climbing up to the high ground overlooking Portsmouth, the naval dockyards and the broad expanse of Portsmouth harbour, once full of warships. Along the heights are a string of fortifications built by Palmerston in the1860s to protect the coast from an invasion by the French.

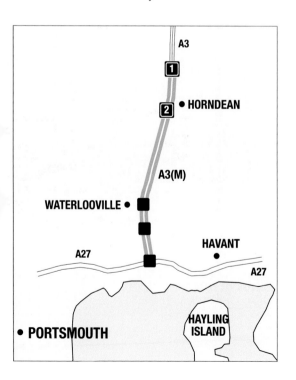

2   Horndean
    Cowplain B2149

Coming from the north take the slip road to Horndean. Get on again at Junction 2 further south. It could be a little complicated.

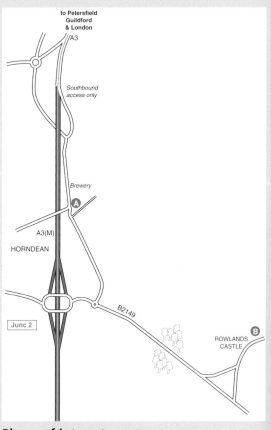

Places of interest
Stansted Park (HHA).

2	Horndean Cowplain B2149

A **The Ship and Bell Hotel.**
Horndean
☎ 02392 592 107
Last orders: 2.30pm and 9.30pm.
No evening meals on Sundays.
_ff_

It has been a coaching inn since 1671 and
was probably the last stop for Nelson's
officers before joining their ships. It has
14 bedrooms, a restaurant, two bars and
serves home cooked fare. A
traditional old English hotel,
which has seen
kinder days.
A comfort stop.

B **The Robin Hood**
Rowlands Castle
☎ 02392 412 268
Last orders: 2.00pm and 9.00pm.
fff *

It has recently opened as a restaurant and
is just within five minutes from the
junction. A friendly atmosphere, light and
airy, looking out over the village green.
Outside seating where children and dogs
are welcome.

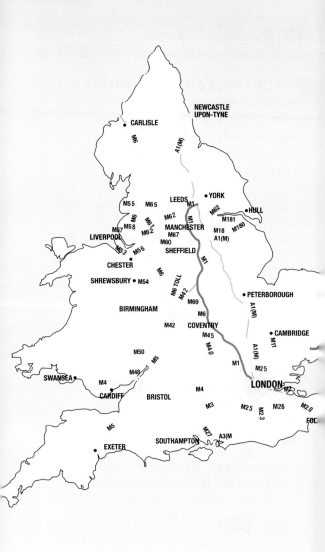

M1

London to Leeds

M1

 9 to **48**

The M1 was the first major motorway to be built in the U.K. The first section of 72 miles was built by Messrs Laing & Son at a cost of £50 million and was completed in 19 months. It was opened in November 1959 by the then Minister of Transport, Ernest Marples, who in real life was a director of a building contracting firm. On the day of the opening an elderly woman crashed her fast Mercedes sports car which resulted in the immediate imposition of speeding restrictions. The final link of the M1, from Leeds to the A1(M) of about 9 miles, was completed in 1999 at a cost of £190 million.

SOUTHERN SECTION

9 to **18**

A congested section of the motorway until past the junction with the M6.

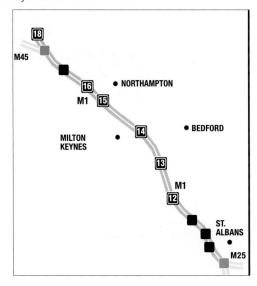

12 — Houghton Regis Woburn Flitwick A5120

Toddington is an attractive village with a large green. There are several other pubs in addition to those mentioned. Harlington is harder to find as it is signposted only as Harlington Station.

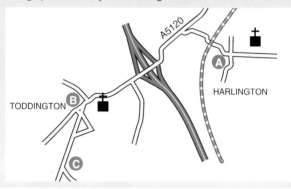

Ⓐ The Carpenters Arms
Harlington
☎ 01525 872 384
Last orders: 2.00pm and 9.00pm. No food on Sunday evenings Closed Mondays.
££

A cheerful low beamed village pub, with a beer garden outside and a pool table inside.

12 Houghton Regis Woburn
Flitwick A5120

The Bell
Toddington
☎ 01525 872 564
Last orders: 3.00pm and 10.00pm.
No evening meals on Friday, Saturday
and Sunday.
ff

it is a popular village pub overlooking the
green with small areas for eating and a bar.
Home cooking and a
cheerful atmosphere.
Outside seating and a
car park at the rear.
Children welcome.

The Angel
Toddington
☎ 01525 872 380
Last orders: 10.30pm.
ff

Reputed to date from the 16th century it is
owned by Greene King and has moved into the
modern age. Bar snacks are available, as is
morning coffee and
tea. There is some
outside seating.
Disabled facilities.
Dogs allowed.

| 13 | Milton Keynes (S) Bedford A421 Ampthill A507   Woburn |

The A4102 to Woburn passes through pleasant countryside. Aspley Guise is an attractive village.

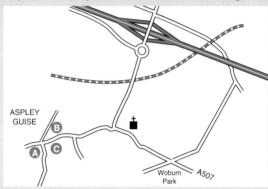

Places of interest
Woburn Abbey (HHA).
Bletchley Park.

 # Moore Place Hotel
Aspley Guise
☎ 01908 282 000
Last orders: 1.45pm and 9.30pm. No lunch on Saturdays.
£££   🛏

A privately owned hotel in a Georgian house built in 1786. It has 64 bedrooms mostly in two modern annexes, as well as The Greenhouse Restaurant and a bar.
Children and dogs welcomed.
Facilities for the disabled.
Breakfasts for the
passing motorists.

13 Milton Keynes (S) Bedford A421
Ampthill A507   Woburn

B The Anchor
Aspley Guise
☎ 01908 582 177
Last orders: 2.00pm and 9.00pm.
Closed Sunday evenings.
££

It has been a pub for more than 100 years
and is owned by the brewery group
Charles Wells. It serves
coffee and bar meals.
Children, dogs
and coaches are
all welcome.
A comfort stop.

C Aspleys Bar & Restaurant
Aspley Guise
☎ 01908 282 877
Last orders: 9.30pm. 10.00pm on Fridays
and Saturdays. Closed on Sundays and
Bank Holidays.
£££

Built in 1837 as a coaching inn and called
the Bell. It is now a restaurant specialising
in Italian food. Garden and car park at
rear.

14 Milton Keynes
Newport Pagnell A509

A nondescript junction in open countryside.

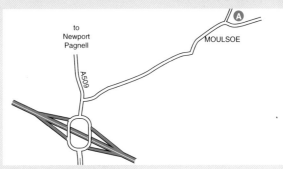

Places of interest
Bletchley Park.
Chicheley Hall (HHA).

 # Carrington Arms
Moulsoe
☎ 01908 218 050
Last orders: 2.30pm and 10.00pm.
9.00 on Sundays
££££   🛏   ✶

Now part of a small group of independent
inns, it specialises in customers choosing their
fish or meat by weight before it is charcoal
grilled in the beamed dining area, served by a
young attentive staff. Bar snacks in the
summer. There are 8
bedrooms in the modern
stable block to the rear.
Dogs in the garden
but children welcome.

15 Northampton (S&E) A508

This junction has been altered recently to give access to a large industrial estate. However it is worth persevering as Collingtree is an attractive village.

Places of interest
Waterways Museum.
Stoke Park Pavilions.

A The Wooden Walls of Old England

Collingtree
☎ 01604 762 427
Last orders: 2.00pm and 9.00pm.
No lunches on Mondays.
£

The name stems from the old beams inside. A pleasant and cheerful atmosphere with log fires, serving real ales. A children's playground and a family room. Dogs allowed outside. A car park and beer garden behind.

16 Northampton Daventry A45

At the junction take the A45 to Daventry. After about two miles is the village of Flore. The Royal Oak is on the left

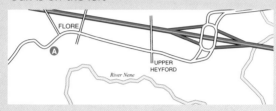

Places of interest
Althorp Hall (HHA).

Ⓐ The Royal Oak
Flore
☎ 01327 341 340
Last orders: 3.00pm and 9.00pm. No evening meals on Sundays and no meals on Tuesdays.
££

An old fashioned pub selling Real Ales to real people. It serves bar meals, but there is a small restaurant area. A large beer garden however and a children's playground, so children and dogs are welcome.

18 Rugby Northampton A428

Pay no attention to the large industrial park to the west but head towards Crick which is a pleasant village.

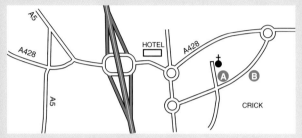

Places of interest
Althorp Hall (HHA).
Stanford Hall.

The Wheatsheaf
Crick
☎ 01788 822 284
Last orders: 2.30pm and 9.00pm.
8.00pm on Sundays.
ff

Records date the building to before 1620, but it has been known as the Wheatsheaf since 1742. It has a restaurant and a bar with a beer garden. Dogs allowed but outdoors. A cheerful atmosphere with traditional ales.

18 Rugby Northampton A428

The Red Lion
Crick
☎ 01788 822 342
Last Orders: 2.00pm and 9.00pm, 9.30 on
Saturdays. No evening meals on Sundays.
ff *

It has been a coaching inn since the early
1700s, but is said to date from the Norman
Conquest.
It is certainly low beamed, as tall visitors will
discover. Some outside seating and a car park
at the rear. A congenial place where they pride
themselves on their Steak Pie served with
traditional ales. Morning coffee available.
Dogs welcome but children at lunch only.

MIDDLE SECTION

19 to **29**

This seems to be a culinary desert with no oasis of peace.

However there are some interesting places to see off the motorway, such as Stanford Hall and the Civil War battlefield of Naseby off Junction 19. At Junction 27 is Lord Byron's old home of Newstead Abbey which he sold in 1816 when he went abroad. Lastly there are those stupendous buildings of Hardwicke Hall, Bolsover Castle, Sutton Scarsdale and further afield, Haddon Hall and Chatsworth.

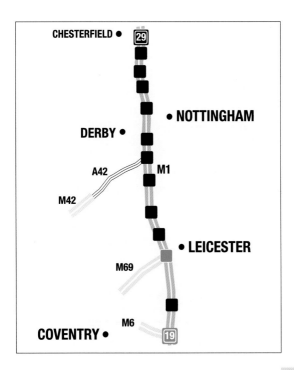

19 Kettering A14

This junction is for the benefit of those driving from the north and going back to the north. However by switching on to the M6 and turning round at Junction 1, you can get to and from Swinford.

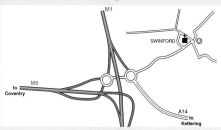

Places of interest
Stamford Hall

A Chequers Inn
Swinford
☎ 01788 860 318
Last Orders: 2.00pm and 9.00pm,
No evening meals on Sundays.
Closed Monday lunch
£

Traditionally friendly village pub with pub games. gas log fires and Real Ale, serving meals in the wood floored bar or in the carpeted dining area. Garden and a playground where dogs and children are welcome.

29 Chesterfield Mansfield A617

This junction is studded with the brown signs of the Tourist Board. The sign to Heath can be missed, which is on the way to the gaunt ruins of Sutton Scarsdale.

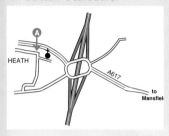

Places of interest
Hardwick Hall (NT).
Bolsover (EH).
Sutton Scarsdale (EH).
Chatsworth (HHA).

Ⓐ **The Elm Tree**
Heath
☎ 10246 850 490
Last orders: 2.00pm and 9.00pm. No evening meals on Sunday and Mondays.
£

Built about a hundred years ago, it is owned by the Wolverhampton and Dudley Brewery and has a non-smoking restaurant and bars. The welcome however is friendly and there is outside seating where you can have a view to the north towards Sutton Scarsdale.   Children and dogs are welcome. A comfort stop.

MIDDLE SECTION

30 to **48**

Certainly not scenic but interesting as you drive through the industrial heartland of this part of England. The places to stop over are equally rare. There are places however to see on the way. These include the Cannon Hall Museum off Junction 37 and near Junction 46 there is Harewood House and Temple Newsam House known as the Hampton Court of the North.

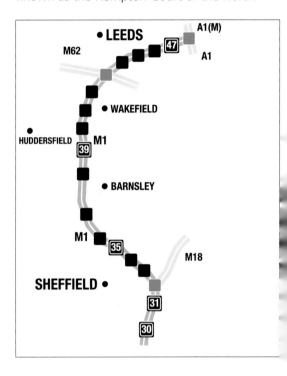

| 30 | Chesterfield Worksop A619 Newark   Sheffield A6135 |

Dual carriageways on each side of the junction but Barlborough is an attractive village when you get off the main road.

Places of interest
Renishaw Hall Gardens (HHA)
Barlborough Hall

 ## The Rose and Crown
Barlborough
☎ 01246 810 364
Last orders: 2.00pm and 8.45pm.
No evening meals on Mondays,Tuesdays and Sundays.
££

The Rose and Crown is signed from the road, and is close to the old church. It has a childrens area and a beer garden. Children allowed if eating with adults and dogs permitted but outdoors. No smoking areas. A comfort stop.

31 Worksop   Sheffield A57

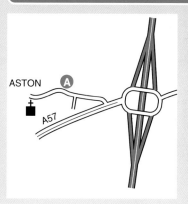

ASTON

A57

A simple junction but look out for the road to Aston cum Aughton, when you come off.

The Yellow Lion

Aston cum Aughton
☎ 01142 872 283
Last orders: 3.00pm and 8.45pm.
No evening meals on Sundays.
£

A locals' pub with stone flagged floors in a fairly built up area, but it overlooks fields. It serves home cooked bar meals and has a children's playground, family room and a beer garden. Dogs allowed. One Armed Bandits and a Pool Table. A comfort stop.

35 Rotherham A629

An easy junction and one turns right almost immediately, as signed.

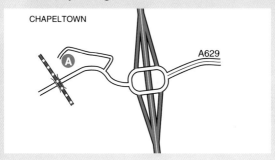

CHAPELTOWN

A629

Ⓐ **The Travellers**
Thorpe Hesley
☎ 01142 467 870
Last orders: 2.30pm and 8.30pm.
No evening meals on Sunday and Monday evenings.
£

A surprise, as it is deep in a wood just off the motorway. It has recently been repainted and renovated and has a large garden at the rear with a childrens playground. Bar meals served. Children and dogs welcome. An outside WC.
A comfort stop.

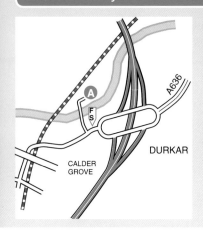

A fairly unimpressive part of the country, but redolent of its industrial past, especially the part played by waterborne transport.

Ⓐ **The Navigation**
Caldergrove
☎ 01924 274 361
Last orders: From noon to 8.00pm.
£

It is situated on the banks of the Calder and Heble Navigation. Owned now by Punch Pub Co, it was once the Dock Masters house, and judging from the photographs on the walls, an inn for boatmen. It serves bar meals and there is a large beer garden and play area on the banks of the canal, where children and dogs are welcome. A comfort stop.

47 Garforth A642 Tadcaster B1217
The North   Wetherby   York A64

The last junction on the M1 before it merges
with a short section of the new A1 Motorway.
Aberford is an attractive village on the old Great
North Road but
now bypassed.

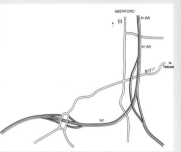

Places of interest
Lotherton Hall.

 ## The White Swan Hotel

Aberford
☎ 01132 813 205
Last orders: 2.30pm and 9.30,pm
10.30pm on Friday and Saturday nights.
££

It has been a coaching inn since 1720,
when the Great North Road passed
outside it. A rusting sign says that J.
Heaton is licensed to rent post horses. It is
a popular, noisy place full of momentoes
and stuffed foxes. No dogs.
A comfort stop.

M2

London to Canterbury

2 to **7**

One of the shorter motorways, being 25 miles in length and was one of the first to be built in 1963. It was designed to make a fast link between London and the Channel Ports, although the approach to London remained abysmal. It has now been supplanted by the M20, with which you can interchange easily should the traffic become unbearable. There are major construction works by Rochester, so the M2 is best avoided for the time being.

The motorway passes near some historic towns such as Rochester; the old Naval Dockyards at Chatham burnt by the Dutch and to the east the ancient city of Canterbury.

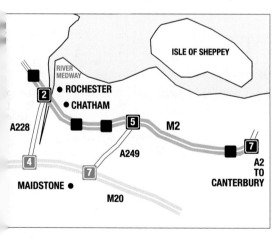

2   Rochester   West Malling
A228

At present it is the scene of construction work,
building the Eurostar bridge over the Medway and
the new railtrack.

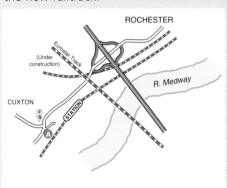

Places of interest
Rochester Castle (EH).
Gads Hill Place (HHA). Chatham Dockyard(EH).

Ⓐ **White Hart**
Cuxton
☎ 01634 711 857
Last orders: 2.30pm and 9.30pm.
No evening meals on Sundays.
££

A managed pub of Shepherd Neame, it has a
restaurant and bars serving bar meals. There is
a playground and a beer garden where dogs
can sit and children play.
A comfort stop.

5 — Maidstone Sheerness A249
The West (M20 & M25)

Easy enough to get to Stockbury, as there is a gap in the dual-carriageway, opposite the turning off.

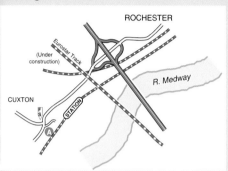

Stockbury features in the Domesday Book as Stochinberge in 1086.

The Harrow Inn
Stockbury
☎ 01795 842 546
Last orders: 2.00pm and 9.30pm.
£££

This typical country pub opposite the village green has been there since 1750. It is a Free House and serves cheerful bar meals and Hurlimann Swiss lager every day of the week. There is a beer garden at the rear where dogs and children can roam.

7 Canterbury A2

The last junction on the motorway before it becomes a dual carriageway to Dover. If you are coming from London there is no difficulty in getting to Boughton and rejoining the Dover road on the other side of the village. Coming from Dover, you can either drive up to the roundabout and return, or else bear off the A2 about 2 miles to the south. Boughton is an attractive village with old half-timbered houses in the vernacular style of the Weald.

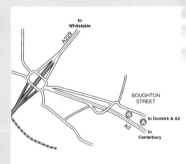

 The Queens Head.

Boughton.

☎ 01227 751 369

Last orders: 2.30pm and 9pm. No evening meals on Sundays and Mondays.

_££_

There has been an inn on the site for the past 400 years and it is still the locals' pub. It serves bar meals, which could be useful if you are too early for the ferry. You can also pass the time of day playing Bat and Trap, a Kentish game. Dogs welcome. A comfort stop.

The Garden Hotel and Restaurant

Boughton

☎ 01227 751 411

Last orders: 2.00pm and 9.00pm.
No evening meals on Sundays.

££　🛏

An old 18th Century house, which was a soup kitchen in the World War II, then an antique shop and for the past ten years a hotel with 10 bedrooms a restaurant and bar. It has just recently been refurbished. Soup is still on the menu, but there are a great many other choices from the menu!

M3

London to Southampton

3 to **14**

This motorway connects London with the port of Southampton and with the south west of England by way of the A303.

The building of the continuation of the motorway past Winchester in 1994 meant the cutting of a trench through Twyford Down. This caused massive unrest (and cost) by protesters. It might have been cheaper in the long run to have tunnelled through.

We could find few places to eat in the southern section but Winchester is well worth a visit.

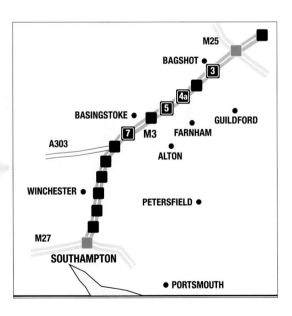

3 Guildford
Bracknell A322 (Woking)

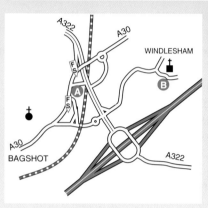

Bagshot has been expanded and therefore you could get lost in the streets. Just keep bearing to the right.

Ⓐ The Barn
Bagshot
☎ 01276 476 673
Last orders: Noon to 9.00pm.
£££

An open beamed barn with a collection of farming artifacts. It is now a restaurant which used to be and probably still is, much frequented by Officer Cadets from Sandhurst. It is family owned, where the food is cooked to order. There is some outside seating, where children are welcome but no dogs.

3 Guildford
Bracknell A322 (Woking)

Half Moon
Windlesham
☎ 01276 473 329
Last orders: 2.15pm and 9.30pm.
No evening meals on Sundays.
£££

A Free House which serves a wide range of traditional food, beers and fruit wines. As a result it has won the Beer and Food Award as well as the Surrey Heath in Bloom Award. Home cooking in the two bars which have a collection of RAF prints. A large beer garden at the back where dogs are welcome.

4a Farnborough (W) A327 Fleet B3013

A simple junction and the pub is easy to find.

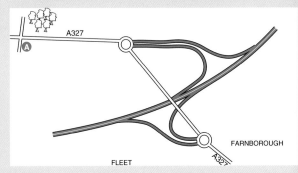

Places of interest
Napoleon III's Mausoleum, Farnborough.
Airborne Forces Museum, Aldershot.

Ⓐ Crown and Cushion
Yateley
☎ 01252 545 253
Last orders: 2.00pm and 8.30pm.
No evening meals on Sundays.
££

An attractive rural pub in a wooded area on the way to Yateley Common. It serves traditional meals in the bars and carvery, or else in the beer garden, which has heaters should the weather be inclement.
Dogs welcome.

5   Farnham A287

No real difficulty with this junction but take the road off the southern roundabout to North Warnborough.

Places of interest
Farnham Castle Keep.
Old Basing House.

Ⓐ **Blubeckers Eating House**
North Warnborough
☎ 01256 702 953
Last orders: 2.30pm and 9.45pm
£££

This was once an old water mill and the mill pond makes an attractive setting for the restaurant, which is a mix of contemporay and olde worlde. There is a playground, a family room and outside seating. Children welcome but no dogs.

7 Basingstoke A30
Newbury (A339)

Not a difficult junction and in fact you can get
from one pub to the other under the Motorway
should one of them be full.

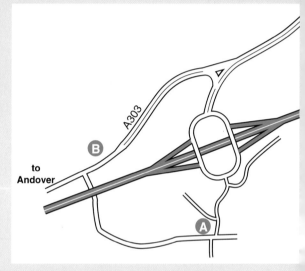

Places of interest
Northington Grange (EH).

Basingstoke A30
Newbury (A339)

Ⓐ Queen Inn
Dummer
☎ 01256 397 367
Last orders: 2.30pm and 9.30pm.
9.00pm on Sundays.
£££ ✶

A popular and well known family owned
pub. It gets its name from the fourth wife
of Henry VIII who was Anne of Cleves,
the Mare of
Flanders. There
is a garden
at the back
where dogs
are welcome.

Ⓑ Sun Inn
Nr Dummer
☎ 01256 397 234
Last orders: 2.30pm and 9.00pm
9.30pm on Fridays and Saturdays.
££

Once a Coaching inn on the old Andover
road, it is now owned by a group and
modernised. It has outside seating and a
beer garden where
dogs and children
are welcome.
A comfort
stop.

M4

London to South Wales

M4

5 to **48**

The M4, which is 121 miles long, is the fourth longest motorway in the UK. It is a direct link from London to South Wales and interconnects with the M5 north of Bristol. The first section, the Chiswick Flyover, was opened in 1959 by a blonde starlet, and the last part to be completed was in 1973. It may be continued to Fishguard at some future date, instead of terminating in a rather bleak part of South Wales. It passes through some of the most varied scenery in Southern England.

EASTERN SECTION **8/9** to **14**

This section of the motorway follows along the Thames valley past Reading and Newbury before rising up to the open expanses of the Marlborough Downs.

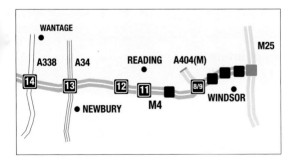

8/9 Maidenhead Windsor A308
Bracknell A308
Henley High Wycombe A4(M)

Coming off at the junction take the motorway
spur to the roundabout. Then follow the signs to
Holyport and turn left at the village green. The
Belgian Arms is on the left at the end of the
green.

For the Shire Horse, take the A404 (M) and turn
left at the roundabout.

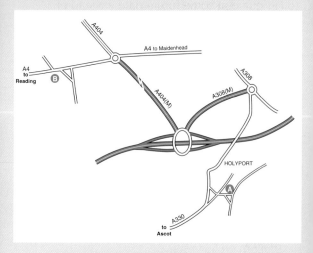

Places of interest
Dorney Court (HHA).
Windsor Castle (Her Majesty The Queen).

| **8/9** | Maidenhead Windsor A308
Bracknell A308
Henley High Wycombe A4(M) |

Ⓐ The Belgian Arms

Holyport
☎ 01628 634 468
Last orders: 2.00pm and 9.30pm.
No evening meals on Sundays.
£££

On the edge of the village green by a duck
pond which ducks still use.
There is a large garden
by the pond where
you can sit in
the summer and
dogs can play.

Ⓑ The Shire Horse

Littlewick Green
☎ 01628 825 335
Last orders: 10.00pm.
9.00pm on Sundays.
££

The pub, part of Scottish and Newcastle,
has open beamed and brick areas serving
bar meals. Outside there is a beer garden
and children's playground. No dogs.
Facilities for the disabled.

11 — Basingstoke A33 / Reading

At the roundabout turn left to Three Mile Cross, but avoid getting onto the dual carriageway.

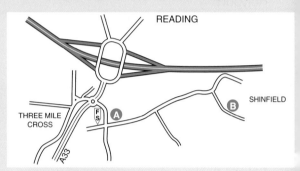

Places of interest
Stratfield Saye (HHA).
Silchester (Calleva Atrebartum).

Ⓐ The Swan

Three Mile Cross
☎ 01189 883 674
Last orders: 10.00pm.
££

Traditional Free House with a restaurant for lunches on weekdays, as well as serving bar meals washed down with Real Ales. There is some outside seating and a beer garden beyond the large car park. The resident Irish Wolfhound, Jumbo, is the mascot of the London Irish Rugby Football Club.

11 Basingstoke A33
Reading

L'Ortolan Restaurant
Shinfield
☎ 01189 883 783
Last orders: 2.30pm and 10.00pm.
No evening meals on Sundays.
££££ *

It was once an old vicarage with a large garden but has now been converted into a comfortable, Michelin starred restaurant, specialising in classical French cuisine. It is efficient with attentive service and is comfortably furnished. A conservatory where you can have a drink before lunch or coffee afterwards.

12 Theale
Reading A4

At the roundabout turn right to Theale, which is a surprisingly attractive little town. It is so named as it was the second night's stop out of London for wagoners and was called The Ale. It certainly seems to have more than its fair share of pubs and hotels, so if the one mentioned below is full, there are probably alternatives.

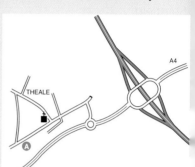

Places of interest

Engelfield House Garden (HHA).
Basildon Park (NT).

 ## The Volunteer
Theale
☎ 01189 302 489
Last orders: Noon to 9.00pm
2.30pm on Sundays.
££

Traditional old pub, serving bar meals with its home cooking. There is outside seating and a car park at the rear. An interesting collection of military and sporting prints.
No dogs indoors.

> **13** Oxford Newbury A34

Ye Olde Red Lion is easy to find. For the Red House follow the plan as indicated and keep going.

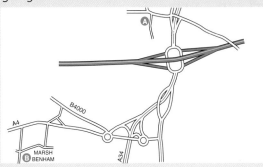

Places of interest
Didcot Railway Centre

Ye Olde Red Lion
Chieveley
☎ 01635 248 379
Last orders: 2.30pm and 9.30pm.
££

An award winning village pub. It has a restaurant with an imaginative menu and a bar with a collection of curios. Log fires inside and benches outside for those wanting fresh air. Children and dogs are welcome but there is a resident dog.

The Red House

Marsh Benham
☎ 01635 582 017
Last orders: 2.15pm and 10.00pm.
No evening meals on Sunday.
Lunch only on Mondays.
££££   ✳

A privately owned elegant restaurant in a thatched house, with an adjoining bar. Outside seating in a garden and its own carpark. They specialise in fish tinged with French cuisine as the manager is a Breton. Children and dogs welcome but preferably outside. Well worth the additional minutes to get there.

14 Hungerford   Wantage A338

An easy junction. Follow the sign to Lambourn for the Pheasant Inn.

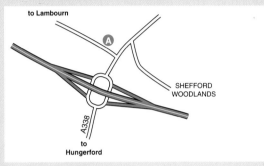

Places of interest
Ashdown House (NT)

The Pheasant Inn
Shefford Woodlands
☎ 01488 648 284
Last orders: 2.30pm and 9.00pm.
9.30pm on Fridays and Saturdays.
Open Sunday evenings.
£££

An historic wooden framed building. It has always been a popular rendezvous and has recently been renovated. It includes a restaurant with an excellent chef, so food is taken seriously but bar snacks are available. It is a pleasant stopover, especially for the racing fraternity. Outside seating in a garden.

MIDDLE SECTION **15** to **23**

This part of the motorway descends from the open chalk Downs towards Junction 15 and Swindon. From there the countryside is typical of the Cotswolds with drystone walls and honey coloured buildings as far as the Severn Bridge.

Swindon was the centre of the locomotive workshops for the Great Western Railway but is now a modern commercial town with a railway museum. Chippenham was once a picturesque market town but has now been modernised out of all recognition. Bath, off Junctionn 18, is famous for its Georgian architecture. The old docks and SS Great Britain in Bristol are also worth a visit.

In 1996 the second Severn Bridge was completed to cope with the increased traffic. The older bridge crossing was then renamed the M48 and the new section became the M4. The M49 link to Avonmouth is best avoided if seeking a meal.

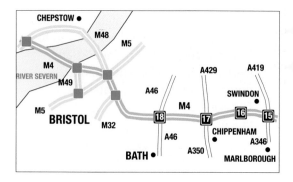

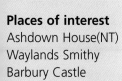

15 Swindon A419
Marlborough A364

There is a clutch of pubs in this area, who probably did a roaring trade when Chiseldon was an airforce base, and then an American military hospital.

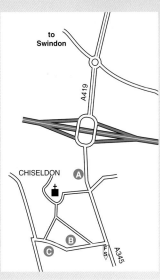

Places of interest
Ashdown House(NT)
Waylands Smithy
Barbury Castle

Plough Inn
Badbury
☎ 01793 740 342
Last orders: 2.00pm and 9.00pm.
££

Pleasant busy wayside pub dating from 1864 owned by Arkells Brewery. It has a restaurant and a bar, childrens playground, beer garden and its own car park. Coffee is available for the passing motorist. Dogs are welcome.

15 Swindon A419
Marlborough A364

B Chiseldon House Hotel
Chiseldon
☎ 01793 741 010
Last orders: 2.00pm and 9.15pm.
£££ 🛏

A fine 19th Century manor house, which
became a privately owned hotel about ten
years ago. It has 21 bedrooms, extensive
gardens and a peaceful setting. Children and
dogs are welcome.
It has the Orangery
Restaurant and a bar.
Morning coffee for
the casual visitor.

C Patriots Arms
Chiseldon
☎ 01793 740 331
Last orders: 2.00pm and 9.00pm
££ 🛏

It has been a pub since 1840 and is now a Free
House with 2 bedrooms, a restaurant and bar.
Outside there is a beer garden and a children's
playground. Inside there is a family room for
wet days. A large
carpark at rear.
Dogs however
are not
welcome.

London to South Wales

16 Swindon   Wootton Bassett
Calne A3102

An uninspiring junction but easy enough to find
the pub, which is before you get into Wootton
Bassett.

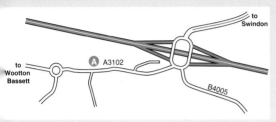

Places of interest
Lydiard Park (Swindon B.C.).

Sally Pussey's Inn
Nr Wootton Bassett
☎ 01793 852 430
Last orders: 8.00am to 9.30pm.
_££_ Breakfast

Do not be too put off by the formidable
woman portrayed on the inn sign, as the
welcome inside is friendly. It has been
modernised to have a Steak and Carvery
Restaurant as well as a bar, which also serves
meals. Breakfast from 8am.
A comfort stop.

17	Chippenham A350 Cirencester A429

Most of the pubs are easy to find, but the Hit and Miss in Kington Langley could be missed which would be a pity. Take the narrow road when you come off the roundabout.

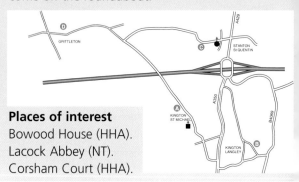

Places of interest
Bowood House (HHA).
Lacock Abbey (NT).
Corsham Court (HHA).

 The Jolly Huntsman
Kington St Michael
☎ 01249 750 305
Last orders: 2.00.pm and 10.00pm
9.00pm on Sundays.
ff 🛏

A popular locals' pub in this attractive village. Well known for its Real Ales of which there are at least 6 different varieties. There are 6 double bedrooms above for those who might wish to drink to the full. Log fires and home made bar meals. Some outside seating and dogs are welcomed by the amiable owners, who stay open for 365 days of the year.

| 17 | Chippenham A350
Cirencester A429 |

B The Hit and Miss

Kington Langley
☎ 01249 758 830
Last orders: 2.30pm and 9.30pm.
8.30pm on Sundays.
££ *

A popular village pub dating from the 18th
Century in the middle of this scattered
hamlet. There is a friendly welcome to all
including dogs and it has an imaginative
menu. A good ambiance.
Some outside
seating for summer
use. It specialises
in sea food.

C Stanton Manor Hotel

Stanton St Quintin
☎ 01666 837 552
Last orders: 2.00pm and 9.30pm
££ 🛏 *

A privately owned hotel, set in 7 acres of
garden. With 23 bedrooms, most in a
modern annexe. Children and dogs by
arrangement. Bar meals are served but
there is the Burghley Restaurant,
so named as the
house was once
owned by Queen
Elizabeth's
Chief Minister.

17 Chippenham A350
Cirencester A429

Neeld Arms
Grittleton
☎ 01249 782 470
Last orders: 2.00.pm and 9.30pm
£££   🛏

A Free House which has recently been taken over by Charlie West. It is a locals village pub but is being improved with two Portuguese chefs dealing with traditional meals with hints of the Iberian peninsula. 6 comfortably furnished bedrooms, one of them in the attic space under a tangle of roof trusses. A cheerful and friendly place and ideal for those coming to Marv Howard's Gift Fair in Hullavington.

18 Bath Stroud A46

An easy junction and not difficult to find the various places.

Places of interest
Dyrham Park(NT).
Horton Court (NT).

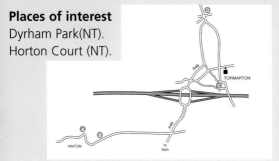

 Hinton Grange Hotel
Hinton
☎ 01179 372 916
Last orders: 2.00.pm and 9.15pm
££££ 🛏 Breakfast

Once a farmhouse built in 1614 and enlarged in 1750, it is surrounded by a lake and garden. It could be described as a querky experience in comfort, to include open fires in the bedrooms of which there are 19. It has a restaurant, a bar in the conservatory and every creature comfort. Dogs are welcome, as are passing motorists at breakfast time.

18 Bath　Stroud A46

Ⓑ Bull Inn
Hinton
☎ 01179 372 332
Last orders: 2.00.pm and 9.30pm
No meals on Sundays
_£££_

A typical village pub with a cheerful
atmosphere. There is a no
smoking restaurant,
outside seating,
a garden and
children's playground.
Dogs are welcome
as are children.

Ⓒ The Portcullis Inn
Tormarton
☎ 01454 218 263
Last orders: 2.30pm and 9.45pm
_££_ 🛏

A friendly, old fashioned, privately owned
village pub, with 6 bedrooms. There is a
dining area and a bar which serves an
excellent Steak and Kidney pie, so much so
that it is now an essential stopping off point
for Czech tourists.
The resident
dog is not too
keen on
canine visitors.

18 Bath   Stroud A46

Cross Hands Hotel
Old Sodbury
☎ 01454 313 000
Last orders: 2.30pm and 10.30pm.
10.00pm on Sundays.
£££ 🛏

An old Coaching Inn which used to be a livery
stable for those coming down for a day out
with the Beaufort Hunt. It is an ingenious mix
of new and old and some of the 15 bedrooms
still reflect those bygone days, as not all of
them have bathrooms attached. There is a
restaurant and bars where morning coffee and
teas are still served. A claim to fame is that the
Queen had to spend the night there in 1981
when marooned in a snow storm. Dogs are
welcome, especially Corgis.

WELSH SECTION   **23a** to   **48**

As the map suggests there are few places where it is worth leaving the motorway to eat. There are however plenty of places to see off the motorway. Caerleon off Junction 24 is the site of Isca, the Roman base of the II (Augusta) Legion from Spain. In Cardiff, the regional capital of Wales, the Castle is built on the walls of the Roman fort whilst to the north there is Castell Coch both restored by the 3rd Marquis of Bute in the nineteenth century with the help of the architect William Burges. Some six miles beyond Castell Coch to the east are the imposing ruins of Caerphilly Castle, mute evidence of the occupation by Edward I.

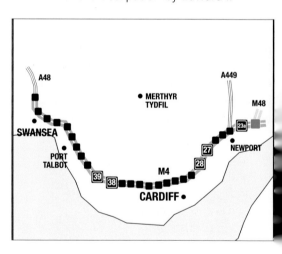

23a Magor B4245

A slightly complicated junction. The approach to the village can confuse the direction to the pub.

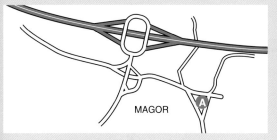

Places of interest
Penhow Castle (HHA).

Ⓐ Wheatsheaf
Magor
☎ 01633 880 608
Last Orders: Noon to 9.30pm.
3.00pm on Sundays.
£ 🛏

Some two hundred years old, it has a large modernised open plan restaurant and bars downstairs where home made food is served. Upstairs there are 5 bedrooms. Some outside seating. Dogs are not permitted.

27   High Cross   B4591

Take the B4591 road north to Risca abd Abertillery.
Afetr about a mile the Rising Sun is on the left.

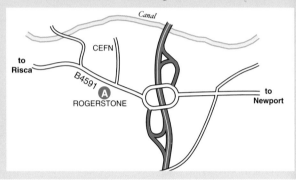

Ⓐ **The Rising Sun**
Rogerstone
☎ 01633 895 126
Last Orders: 2.15pm and 9.00pm.
No evening meals on Sundays.
££

A tenanted pub with an enterprising manager.
He has built a two storey conservatory at the
rear of the restaurant, with two large bars
elsewhere. The menu is imaginative on a self
serve basis. Children welcome. A surprise to
find a deservedly popular place which looks at
first sight unassuming.

---

28 Newport A48 Caerphilly A468

Once off the motorway follow the signs to Tredegar House.

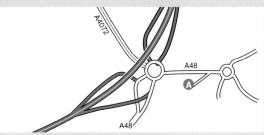

Places of interest
Tredegar House.(HHA)

The Brewhouse Tearoom

Tredegar House
☎ 01633 817 279
Last orders:5.00pm Wednesdays to Sundays.
Closed Mondays and Tuesdays.
£

Tredegar House, which is a member of the HHA, is open to the public from Easter to the end of September. The Brewhouse Tearoom is really a cafe, but serves light lunches as well as morning coffee and cream teas. A slightly different atmosphere from the usual motorway stopover.

38/39   Port Talbot A48

Going east there is no problem about exiting
and entering again, but driving west, you have
to take the dual carriageway for a short
distance before joining the motorway again.

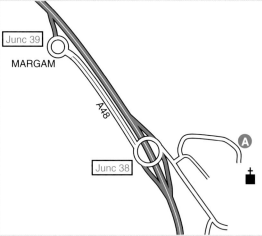

Places of interest
Margam Castle (HHA).
The Stones Museum.
Margam Abbey.

38/39 Port Talbot A48

The Abbots Kitchen and Restaurant

Margam
☎ 01639 871 184
Last orders: 4.00pm. 2.30pm on Sundays.
£

A haven of peace shielded from the steel works in Port Talbot by woodland. The whole area was part of an Early Norman abbey. The church was 'restored' by the Victorians, but nevertheless it is still a fine building, where services are held. Nearby is the Stones Museum with a good collection of inscribed Celtic stones.

The Abbots Kitchen is in the stables of what was once Margam House before it was demolished. Tea, coffee and cakes or a light lunch are provided until 4pm.

Dogs and children welcome.

NEWCASTLE
UPON-TYNE

CARLISLE

M6

A1(M)

LEEDS

YORK

M1

M62

HULL

M55

M65

M62

M181

M58

M61

M62

MANCHESTER

M18

M180

M57

M67

A1(M)

LIVERPOOL

M60

M53

M56

SHEFFIELD

CHESTER

M1

SHREWSBURY

M54

M6

PETERBOROUGH

M6 TOLL

M42

A1(M)

BIRMINGHAM

M69

CAMBRIDGE

M6

M11

M42

COVENTRY

M45

M50

M40

A1(M)

M5

M48

M1

M25

SWANSEA

M4

M2

CARDIFF

BRISTOL

LONDON

M5

M4

M25

M26

M20

M3

M23

M5

M27

A3(M)

Fol

EXETER

SOUTHAMPTON

M5

94

Birmingham to Exeter

3 to **31**

The M5 is 168 miles in length and was built in sections, the first part being completed in 1969 and the last in 1976. It was designed to link the Midlands with the South West, via Bristol. It is one of the few Motorways which has no connection with London. Considering that it passes through some of the prettiest of the English countryside, it is poorly served for looking after the needs of motorists.

NORTHERN SECTION **1** to **10**

A boring stretch of motorway until you get south of Worcester.

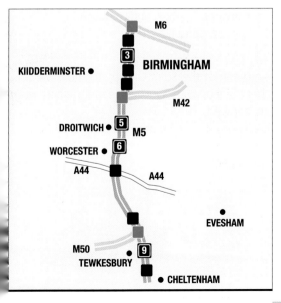

> **3** Birmingham (W and Cen) A456
> Kidderminster

A straightforward junction. Just follow the dual carriageway until you see the pub. You will have to get back to the junction by going round the roundabout.

Places of interest
Haglay Hall (HHA)
Halesowen Abbey.

Ⓐ The Black Horse
Halesowen
☎ 0121 550 1465
Last orders: 2.00pm and 10.00pm.
9.30pm on Sundays.
££

An outlet of the Spirit Group, it is however a cheerful stopover. Outside seating, where dogs are allowed.
It serves in-house created meals in a peaceful atmosphere of (at present) William Morris wallpaper.

Birmingham to Exeter

5 Droitwich Bromsgrove A38

The roundabouts tend to confuse but look out for the signs to Droitwich

Places of interest
Hanbury Hall (NT)

Robin Hood
Rashwood
☎ 01527 861 931
Last orders:9.30pm. 10pm on Saturdays.
9pm on Sundays.
ff

A Bass owned pub, it is well known to the passing motorist. Outside seating and a beer garden at the rear, where dogs are allowed.

Chateau Impney

Nr Droitwich

☎ 01905 774 411

Last orders: 2.00pm and 8.30pm

8.00pm on Sundays

££££   🛏

An amazing French edifice in the middle of England, built by a local salt magnet, Sir John Corbett, in 1875. It is now a privately owned hotel in 150 acres of parkland with 114 bedrooms, restaurants and a carvery. For those in more of a hurry the lounge bars serve sandwiches. There is a golf course nearby for those wishing to work off their lunch. No dogs.

6 Kidderminster A449
Evesham A4538

Follow the plan so as not to overshoot the turning to the right.

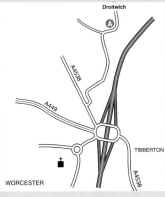

Places of interest

Worcester Cathedral.
Dyson Perrins Museum (Royal Worcester porcelain).
Droitwich Spa.

 The Pear Tree
Smite
☎ 01905 756 565
Last orders: 2.30pm and 9.30pm.
£££ Breakfast

A family owned 24 bedroom hotel and conference centre, which was converted and enlarged some ten years ago. The original house dating from the 18th century is where you can now have bar meals. Fresh fish a speciality. No dogs. Breakfast for the passing traveller.

9 Tewkesbury A438
Evesham A46

A simple junction. Just keep going until you see the tower of the Abbey. It is a picturesque old market town with some fine buildings.

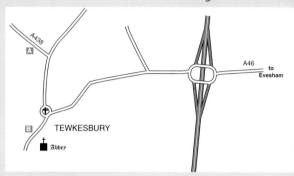

Places of interest
Tewkesbury Abbey

Ⓐ Ye Olde Black Bear
Tewkesbury
☎ 01684 292 202
Last orders: 9.00pm.
No evening meals on Sunday.
££

Said to be the oldest pub in Gloucestershire, dating from 1308. It has a beer garden at the rear on the banks of the Lower Avon Navigation Canal where dogs are allowed. Bar meals are served throughout the day.

Tewkesbury A438
Evesham A46

The Royal Hop Pole
Tewkesbury
☎ 01684 293 236
Last orders: 2.00pm and 9.00pm.
9.30pm on Fridays and Saturdays.
No evening meals on Sundays.
£££

It is a comfortable old fashioned hotel. No one
seems to know the origin of the name but it
dates from the 15th century. It is also famous
as the place where Dickens wrote that Pickwick
spent the night there! There are 29 bedrooms,
most facing onto a well tended garden leading
down to the river Avon. A restaurant and a
friendly bar looks after the inner man, or
should one say person.

MIDDLE SECTION **11a** to **21**

This stretch takes you from Gloucester, with its historic cathedral where Edward II is buried and Cheltenham, to south of Bristol. The motorway passes through pleasant countryside and there are interesting houses and places to see along the River Severn. After the crossing with the M4, Junction 18 is the best turn off for Bristol, after passing Kings Weston, designed by Sir John Vanbrugh. You can drive along the Avon Gorge, under Brunel's Clifton Suspension Bridge and then into Bristol with its restored dockside including the SS Great Britain.

During the summer the stretch from the M4 intersection and the bridge over the Avon can get gridlocked.

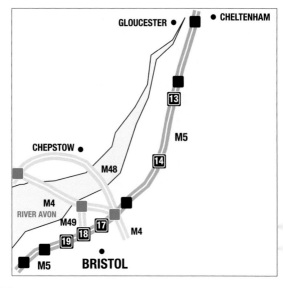

13 Stroud A419
Dursley

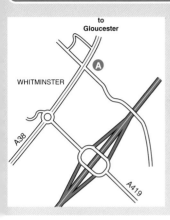

An easy junction.

Places of interest
Hardwicke Court (HHA).
Wildfowl and Wetlands Centre (Slimbridge).
Frampton Manor.

Ⓐ The Old Forge

Whitminster
☎ 01452 741 306
Last orders: 2.00pm and 9.00pm.
No evening meals on Sundays and Mondays
££   *

The building is dated 1604 and must have been a smithy if the name is to be believed. It is a Free House and has a cheerful and friendly atmosphere with a small low beamed but airy restaurant. There is outside seating and dogs are welcome.

> **14**   Thornbury
> Dursley B4509

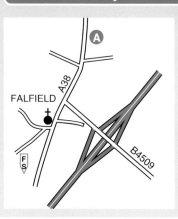

An uncomplicated junction.

Places of interest
Berkeley Castle (HHA).

(A)

The Gables
Falfield
☎ 01454 260 502
Last orders: 2.00pm for bar meals only.
9.30pm in the bar and restaurant.
£££   🍴   Breakfast

The Gables was once a wayside pub. It has now been rebuilt as an hotel with 46 bedrooms, a restaurant, bar (where Charfield Real Ale is served) and fitness gym for those wanting a workout or relaxing from a conference. Breakfast for passing motorists.

Birmingham to Exeter

17 Bristol Clifton A4018

Easy enough to find the way, especially if in need of a comfort stop. Good view towards the Severn Bridges.

The Fox
Easter Compton
☎ 01454 632 220
Last orders: 2.00pm and 9.30pm.
No evening meals on Sundays.
££

A village pub with a garden and children's playground. Morning coffee can be had if in a rush. Under 14s not allowed in the bars. A comfort stop.

18   Avonmouth
Bristol   A4

The exit is complicated as it gets snarled up with
the junction of the M49. Follow the A4 Portway
sign. At Shirehampton turn left up Kings Weston
Avenue. After passing the remains of a Roman Villa
on the right, turn right up the hill marked Kings
Weston Lane. The entrance gates are at the top of
the hill on the right. You can see the amazing
chimneys of the house from the motorway

Places of interes
SS Great Britain
Bristol Docks

Ⓐ Kings Weston House

Kings Weston
☎ 01179 382 299
Last orders: 10am to 4pm every day.
£   ✳

It is not every motorist who can have a light
lunch or a traditional tea in a house designed
by Sir John Vanbrugh. It has now been
renovated to cater for conferences and
functions. The Tea Room below,
complete with a Vanbrugh
fireplace, is open
to passing motorists.
There is a large
park for walking
the dog.

19 Clifton
Portishead A369

The Rudgeleigh Inn is easy to find, but the Priory, will require more effort, especially as the approach road is narrow.

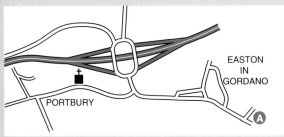

Rudgeleigh Inn
Easton in Gordano
☎ 01275 372 363
Last orders: 10.00pm.9.30pm on Sundays.
££

It is a family owned pub, with a large collection of jugs hanging from the beams in the eating areas where meals are served. There is outside seating where children and dogs are more than welcome.

SOUTHERN SECTION 22 to 31

South of Bristol the motorway winds between
the Mendip Hills before crossing the flat levels
of Sedgemoor, remembered for the defeat of
the Duke of Monmouth and the Bloody Assizes
of Judge Jeffreys.

Glastonbury famous for the supposed site of
the Holy Grail and also for the annual pop
concerts is close to the motorway.

Taunton is an attractive county town, with a
good antique market. The motorway ends
south of Exeter, which was once a Roman city,
with a fine medieval cathedral. It continues as
a dual- carriageway to Plymouth and Cornwall.

Birmingham to Exeter

> **23** Bridgwater A38
> Glastonbury   Wells (A39)

The Puriton Inn is signed just off the junction
on the left.

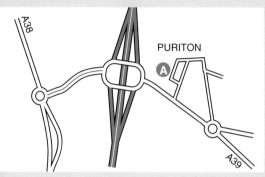

Places of interest
Glastonbury Abbey.
Wells Cathedral.

The Puriton Inn
Puriton
☎ 01278 683 464
Last orders: 2.30pm and 9.30pm.
9.00pm on Sundays.
£

A 200 year old village pub with a Skittle Alley.
It takes a pride in its home cooking. There is a
children's playground and outside seating,
where dogs are permitted.
Car park.

---

24 Bridgewater A38
Minehead

The junction is easy enough, but the road to
Huntworth is twisty and narrow - keep on over a
narrow wooden bridge.

Places of interest
Maunsel Grange Garden (HHA).

A The Boat and Anchor Inn
Huntworth
☎ 01278 662 473
Last orders: May-Oct.From noon-9.00pm
Oct-May. 3,00 & 9.00pm
££

The reason for the name soon becomes
apparent as the beer garden is on the banks of
the Bridgewater and Taunton Canal. It has 3
bedrooms which are double glazed, a
restaurant and a long bar. Coffee is served to
thirsty bargees as well as something stronger.
Children and dogs are welcome, if kept on a
lead.

| 24 | Bridgewater A38
Minehead |

The Compass Tavern

North Petherton
☎ 01278 662 283
Last orders: 2.45pm and 8.45pm.
9.30pm on Fridays and Saturdays.
ff

A 16th century pub, which specialises in home cooking in a large open beamed dining area but pay heed to the notices to mind your step or mind your head. Large beer garden. Children allowed.

25 Taunton Honiton Yeovil Weymouth A358

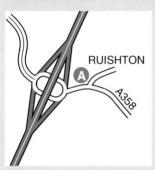

RUISHTON

A

A358

An easy junction being the main turn off for Taunton. Follow the signs to Ilminster, and the Blackbrook Tavern is to the left, just off the roundabout.

Places of interest
Hestercombe House Gardens (HHA).

A Blackbrook Tavern

Ruishton
☎ 01823 443 121
Last orders: 10.00pm. 9.30pm on Sundays.
££ 🛏 Breakfast

A popular and busy pub of beams and bricks, on the outskirts of Taunton, with 38 double bedrooms, a restaurant and bars. There is a children's playground as well as outside seating. Dogs are not welcome. Breakfasts available.

Birmingham to Exeter

> **26** **Wellington A38**
> **Taunton**

Turn right on the roundabout on the A38. Wellington is a pleasant country town but nothing special in the way of places to eat. The return to the motorway from the Blackbird via West Buckland is not recommended, as the roads are narrow and you could get lost.

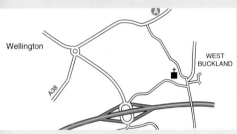

Places of interest Cothay Manor Gardens (HHA)

The Blackbird
West Buckland
☎ 018223 461 273
Last orders: 2.00pm and 9.30pm.
No evening meals on Sundays.
££ 🛏 ✳

A Free House, it prides itself on the home cooking, served in the restaurant with lace table cloths and in the bar. It also has 2 bedrooms for the overnight motorist. Outside there is a beer garden but dog owners are warned that there are two large resident dogs. Children welcome.

113

27 Tiverton Barnstaple A361
Wellington A38

Getting there is easy enough but the return is more difficult with what seems to be a needlessly complicated system of roundabouts.

Places of interest
Knightshayes Court.(NT)

 The Globe Inn

Sampford Peverell
☎ 01884 821 214
Last orders: 2.00pm and 10.00pm.
££ 🛏

A popular pub with a restaurant and bars as well as 6 double bedrooms. There is a children's playground and a beer garden at the rear. Dogs are welcome, and there are facilities for the disabled. A skittle alley for use on wet days.

27 Tiverton Barnstaple A361
Wellington A38

The Parkway House Hotel

Sampford Peverell
☎ 01884 820 255
Last orders: 2.00pm and 10.00pm
£££ 🛏 Breakfast

An unassuming modernish building with a
large garden. It is a family owned and run
hotel with attentive and friendly service. It has
10 bedrooms, an airy conservatory and a
restaurant. Children welcome and dogs by
arrangement. Breakfast for the passing
motorist.

28   Cullompton B3181
      Honiton A373

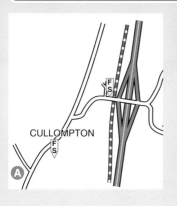

CULLOMPTON

Ⓐ

Slightly complicated by having a Motorway Service Station just off the junction. There is also another filling station on the way into Cullompton, which is an attractive town. You may miss the road back to the motorway by continuing north.

Ⓐ **Manor House Hotel**

Cullompton
☎ 01884 322 281
Last orders: 2.30pm and 9.30pm.
Lunch only on Sundays.
££ 🛏

A 17th Century town house which must once have been of some importance. It is now privately owned with part being a hotel with 9 bedrooms and a restaurant and the other side being a public bar which has not been renovated. Outside seating and a car park at the rear. A comfort stop.

30 Exmouth Sidmouth A376
Dawlish

The village is not difficult to find. To get to the Blue Ball Inn, you will have to go up to the roundabout and return as there is no break in the dual carriageway.

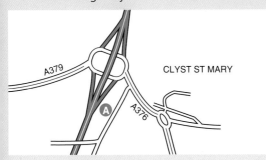

A379

CLYST ST MARY

Ⓐ

A376

Ⓐ Blue Ball Inn
Sandygate
☎ 01392 873 401
Last orders: 2.30pm and 9.30pm
9.00pm on Sundays.
£££   ✳

An attractive 18th Century pub in a quiet lane, with scrubbed tables, tiled floors, low beamed ceilings and home cooking. Coffee and teas can also be had. There is a large garden, but dogs are not welcome. It is about to be enlarged.

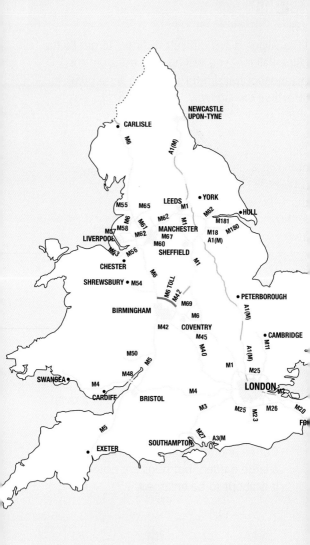

NEWCASTLE UPON-TYNE

CARLISLE

M6

A1(M)

M55
M65
LEEDS
M1
YORK
M62
HULL
M6
M61
M62
M181
MANCHESTER
M57
M58
M62
M67
M18
M180
LIVERPOOL
M63
M56
M60
A1(M)
SHEFFIELD
CHESTER
M1
SHREWSBURY
M54
M6
M6 TOLL
M42
PETERBOROUGH
BIRMINGHAM
M69
A1(M)
M42
M6
M50
COVENTRY
CAMBRIDGE
M45
M11
M5
M40
A1(M)
SWANSEA
M48
M1
M25
M4
CARDIFF
LONDON
M2
BRISTOL
M4
M3
M25
M26
M20
M23
M5
M27
A3(M)
EXETER
SOUTHAMPTON
FO

M6 and M6 (Toll)

M6 (toll)

This is the latest addition to the motorway network and is due to be opened on 1st January 2004. Built by private enterprise under the aegis of the last government, the cost to the public both financially and timewise is yet to be experienced. It must certainly be an improvement to the endless traffic jams at Spaghetti Junction which could add hours to journey times. At first glance the route does not seem to bode well for finding places just off the junctions, but there are some amongst the area north of Birmingham. For golfing enthusiasts there is the De Vere Belfry Hotel just of junction 2, but access there is restricted. Another snag is that to regain access to the motorway you will have to pay another toll charge.

M6 (toll)

4 Lichfield A38

Take the A38 to Lichfield. After about half a mile there is a gap in the central reservation and a sign for Swinfen. Pass two signs – one saying Swinfen Hall Hotel, the other saying Her Majesty's Young Offenders Institute Swinfen or HM.YOI for short. A surprise awaits you.

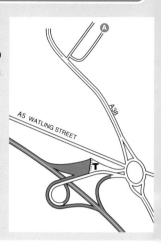

 Swinfen Hall Hotel
Swinfen
☎ 01543 481 494
Last orders: 2.30pm and 9.30pm.
££££ 🛏 Breakfast ★

The original part of the house was built in 1757 to the design of Benjamin Wyatt. The Swinfens lived there until 1948, when it was given to the Local Council and from them to the Government who built the YOI in the grounds and the house became derelict. It has now been converted it into an elegant hotel with 19 bedrooms and a Ballroom. Children welcome but dogs in cars overnight.

5 Sheestone A5127

A simple junction with a Toll Station on the exit only. Take the A5127 to Sheestone and after the first roundabout you will see the Bulls Head on the right hand side.

Ⓐ The Bulls Head
Shenstone
☎ 01543 480 214
Last orders: 10pm every day. 9.30 on Sundays.
££

A managed house of Mitchells and Butlers. It has had a company makeover but still retains a friendly, folksy atmosphere with restaurant areas and bars. Outside seating and a large car park at rear. Children welcome but dogs outside.

1 to **44**

A first trial section of a motorway was built as the Preston Bypass in 1958, before the M1 was finished in 1959. The M6 is one of the longest motorways, being some 180 miles in length. It was built over a period of years, starting in 1962 and the last section was finished in 1972. The link over the Scottish Border connecting up with the M74 is still to be completed.

SOUTHERN SECTION **1** to **14**

This section of the motorway is dull and when combined with the inevitable snarl up at Spaghetti Junction it becomes downright tedious. It gets better just south of Stafford. The opening of the new M6 (Toll) should improve matters.

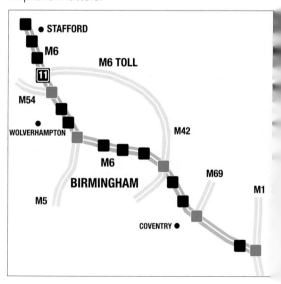

Wolverhampton Cannock A460 Telford (M54)

On the way to Shareshill there is a filling station but it only sells diesel.
For those driving from the north and wanting to go to Shrewsbury, turn off here to get to the M54.
The new M6 (Toll) joins the M6 at Junction 11A some two miles north

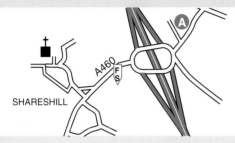

The Wheatsheaf

Laney Green
☎ 01922 412 304
Last orders: 2.00pm and 8.30pm.
Closed Sunday evenings.
££

Once an old road side pub, it has now been modernised, with a conservatory style dining area. Bar meals served. Childrens playground, a garden and plenty of parking.

MIDDLE SECTION 15 to 32

Stoke on Trent is the home of pottery, which is attractive but the same could not be said for the town itself. Nearby Barleston Hall was built in 1756 by Sir Robert Taylor for the Wedgewoods as their home and factory. It was shamefully neglected by the firm until saved at the last moment by SAVE Britain's Heritage.

The countryside in Cheshire is pleasant enough but once over the Manchester Ship Canal, the surroundings are more crowded, mingled with motorways. It is small wonder that the local inhabitants were beginning to complain as more and more of their land was being taken to build yet another motorway.

17 Congleton Sandbach A534

Look out for Church Lane, which is made
obvious by the Church.

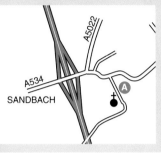

Places of interest
Little Moreton
Hall. (NT)

The Chimney House Hotel
Sandbach
☎ 01270 764 141
Last orders: 2.00pm and 10.00pm,
9.30pm on Sundays.
£££ 🛏

It was once the Rectory, but is now converted
to a modern hotel with 48 bedrooms and a
conference centre with appropriate car parking.
A comfortable restaurant but the lounge bar
also serves snacks. There is outside seating and
eight acres of woodland. Children but no dogs
allowed. Breakfast can be available.

18 Middlewich   Northwich
Chester   Holmes Chapel A54

No difficulty with this junction.

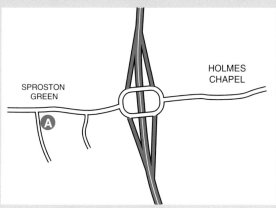

Places of interest
Capesthorne Hall. (HHA)

Ⓐ The Fox and Hounds

Sproston Green
☎ 01606 832 303
Last orders: 2.30pm and 9.00pm.
8.00pm on Sundays. Closed Monday nights.
££

A wayside pub now owned by Pub Mistress. It
has a restaurant and bars with flagged floors,
beamed ceilings and a bowling green now out
of use. A beer garden where children and
dogs are welcome.

19	Manchester A556
	Northwich Knutsford A537

The junction itself is easy but busy, as the A556 feeds in from Cheshire. The Smoker at Plumley may seem to be quite far.

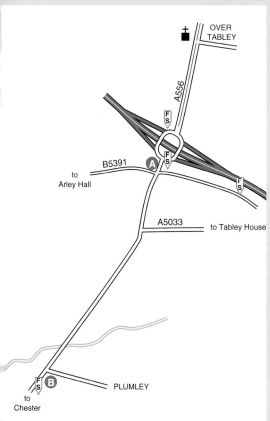

Places of interest
Arley Hall (HHA)
Tatton Park.(NT)
Tabley House.

19	Manchester A556 Northwich Knutsford A537

Ⓐ Windmill Inn
Tabley
☎ 01565 631 993
Last orders: 12.00am to 9.00pm daily.
_££_

A Free House serving traditional Real Ales and
bar meals with real fires. Breakfasts may be
available to motorists. It has its own car park
and is opposite a filling station.
Children and dogs
are welcome.

Ⓑ The Smoker
Plumley
☎ 01565 722 338
Last orders: 2.15pm and 9.30pm.
9.00pm on Sundays.
_££_

Named after a race horse bred by the Prince
Regent. It has a large garden, a comfortable
restaurant, open fires and plenty of seating.
The building is over 400 years old and is
rumoured to have a ghost, so dogs
not welcome.

29 Blackburn A6
Burnley M65

Not an easy junction. Turn right at the traffic lights and bear right at the village green.

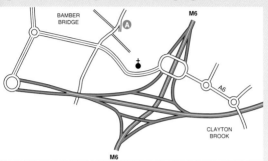

Ye Olde Hob Inn

Bamber Bridge
☎ 01772 336 863
Last orders: 2.00pm and 9.00pm.
Closed on Monday evenings.
££   ✳

A welcome surprise to find an old rustic, thatch roofed traditional pub, although it is owned by Scottish and Newcastle. It has a restaurant as well as a bar, with outside seating and a family room for wet weather. Children but no dogs.

31 Preston Blackburn A59 Clitheroe

Keep your head when negotiating the roundabouts on each side of the motorway.

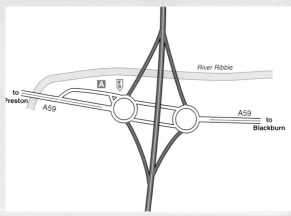

Places of interest

Samlesbury Hall. (Samlesbury Hall Trust).

Ⓐ The Tickled Trout Inn

Nr Samlesbury

☎ 01772 877 671

Last orders: 2.00pm and 9.45pm.

££££

Now part of the Macdonalds hotel chain, it has 72 bedrooms, conference facilities, a leisure centre and a golf course nearby. For those who would like a bar meal and look at the river, there is outside seating. Children and dogs belonging to residents.

Rugby to Carlisle

NORTHERN SECTION 33 to 44

This section is the most scenic of any of the motorways. After Lancaster, which is an interesting county town, the motorway ascends past Kendal, with the the Lake District to the west and the Pennines to the east. Once over Shap, the highest point of the motorway, it descends past Penrith which is a picturesque market town, to Carlisle which is well worth a visit. From there the motorway crosses over the River Esk into Scotland.

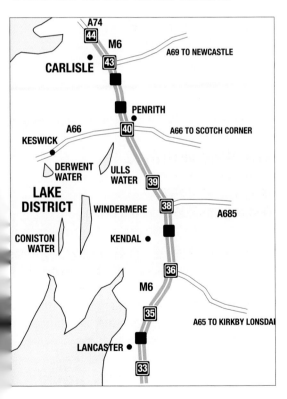

33 Lancaster (S)
Fleetwood   Garstang A6

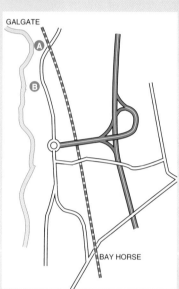

Easy enough to get off the motorway.

GALGATE

BAY HORSE

 A

The Plough Inn

Galgate

☎ 01524 751 337.

Last orders: 2.00pm and 8.00pm.

£

A Free House, with small round tables and wooden flooring. There is a garden with outside seating. Children and dogs, provided they behave themselves.

A comfort stop.

33 Lancaster (S)
Fleetwood   Garstang A6

Canalside Craft Centre
Galgate
☎ 01524 752 223
Last orders: 4.00pm.
££

A craft centre with a coffee shop, serving everything from toast to a full meal. An ideal spot for those just wanting a light or full lunch and an airing for dogs or children along the canal. Home made meals, soups and cakes a speciality.

35 Morecambe (A6)
Carnforth A601(M)

Do not panic about the motorway interchange.
The road to Over Kellet, which is an attractive
village still with its village shop, is easy to follow.

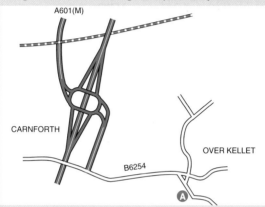

Places of interest
Leighton Hall (HHA)

 # The Eagles Head

Over Kellet
☎ 01524 732 457
Last orders: 2.00pm and 9.00pm.
££

A cheerful country pub owned by Mitchells.
Bar meals served daily in a large dining area
cum bar with exposed stone walls and timber
ceilings. It specialises in home cured and
cooked ham.
It has a children's
room, a
beer garden
and its
own car
park.

36 S.Lakes Kendal Barrow A590
Kirkby Lonsdale Skipton A65

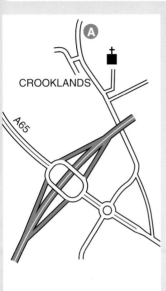

CROOKLANDS

A65

A boring junction with dual carriageways on either side. Look out for the Crookland Hotel signs.

Places of interest
Levens Hall. (HHA)
Sizergh Castle.(NT)

A Crooklands Hotel
Crooklands
☎ 01539 567 432
Last orders: 2.00pm and 9.00pm.
£££

A privately owned hotel with 30 double rooms in a new extension. There is a restaurant and bars as well as a Carvery. Morning coffee for the passing motorist. Children, but no dogs.

38 Brough   Kendal A685
Appleby B6260

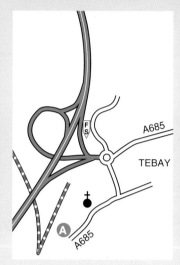

Somewhat complicated with dual carriageways leading off and onto the motorway. After the roundabout, drive through Tebay.

Places of interest
The Roman fort and road at Low Borrowbridge.
(If you can get to it!)

Ⓐ The Cross Keys
Tebay
☎ 01539 624 240
Last orders: 2.30pm and 9.00pm.
££ 🛏 ✳

An old coaching inn on the way to Appleby. It is privately owned with a cheerful and friendly staff. It still caters for motorists with 6 double rooms, a beer garden and the best Steak and Mushroom pies in the area. Children and dogs are welcome, but dogs to be controlled.

39 Shap (A6)
Kendal A6

An easy junction.

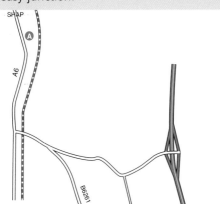

Places of interest
Shap Abbey. (EH)

A The Greyhound Hotel
Shap
☎ 01931 716 4
Last orders: 2.00pm and 9.00pm.
£ ⇔

This was an elegant Georgian coaching
inn, where apparently Bonnie Prince
Charlie spent a night on his way south. It
has however been modernised for pub use
to include copper topped tables in the bar.
It has 18 bedrooms, but beware of the
main railway line just behind.
A comfort stop.

40 — N. Lakes Keswick Penrith A66 Brough A68

A busy junction with traffic coming in from the Lake District or going to Scotch Corner. Penrith was once the crossing point for the coaching traffic going north and south and also for those going to the Cumbrian ports or over the Pennines to Barnard Castle. As a result there is a plethora of old coaching inns and wayside pubs to this day.

The Red Rooster Roadstop, part of the garage at the first roundabout in Penrith does a good breakfast for lorry drivers and others.

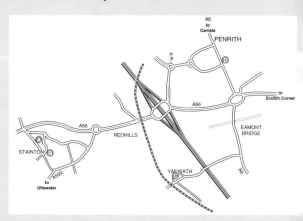

Places of interest

Dalemain (HHA).
Penrith Castle.
The Toffee Shop, Penrith.
King Arthur's Round Table (EH).
Mayburgh Henge (EH)
Hutton in the Forest (HHA).

40 N. Lakes Keswick Penrith A66
Brough A68

Ⓐ The King's Arms
Stainton
☎ 01768 862 778
Last orders: 2.00pm and 9.00pm in the summer. 8.30pm in the winter. Closed all day Mondays.
ff

A pub dating from 1721 in a rural Cumbrian village. It still serves bar meals and a Steak and Kidney pie made to an old recipe. The genial Scots host was a hotelier before becoming a ski instructor.

Ⓑ Brantwood Country Hotel
Stainton
☎ 01768 862 748
Last orders: 2.00pm and 8.45pm.
ff 🛏

A family owned hotel and restaurant with 7 bedrooms and a large garden. An 19th century comfortably furnished house with oak beams and log fires.

40 N. Lakes Keswick Penrith A66
Brough A68

The Yanwath Gate Inn
Yanwath
☎ 01768 862 386
Last orders: 2.15pm to 9.30pm.
9.00pm on Sundays.
ff ✳

A privately owned pub dating from 1683. It is
in a quiet secluded backwater with a restaurant
and bar, as well as a beer garden. It specialises
in fish dishes and home cooking. Dogs and
children allowed. The sign over the door says
"This gate hangs well and hinders none.
Refresh and pay and travel on".

N. Lakes Keswick Penrith A66
Brough A68

The George Hotel
Penrith
☎ 01768 862 696
Last orders: 2.30pm and 10.00pm.
9.30 on Sundays, during the winter.
£££ 🛏

A privately owned hotel in the centre of Penrith
which has been a coaching inn for the past
300 years. It is a fast disappearing example of
old style comfort and service. It is being
refurbished for completion during the coming
year. It has 34 bedrooms, a restaurant and a
bar. The carpark at the rear, where the
carriages used to be, is locked at nights.
Children are permitted and dogs at a charge.

43 Carlisle A6
Hexham Newcastle A69

After coming off the junction there is a stretch of
dual carriageway at the end of which is the
Waterloo. Look out for the sign to Wetheral to the
right which is about a three minute drive. There is
a large green in the village.

For the Queen's Arms Hotel continue on towards
Warwick on Eden and take a slip road to the right.
If you come to the traffic lights on the bridge over
the river Eden you have gone too far.

Places of interest

Carlisle, with its Castle and early Norman Cathedral
Wetheral Priory Gatehouse.
Corby Castle.

 # The Waterloo

Aglionby
☎ 01228 513 347
Last orders: 2.30pm and 8.45pm.
££

A small traditional wayside
pub serving bar meals.
It has a beer garden
and a car park at rear.
Yes to children,
but no to dogs.

| 43 | Carlisle A6
Hexham Newcastle A69 |

B

Queen's Arms Hotel
Warwick on Eden
☎ 01228 560 699
Last orders: 1.45pm and 8.45pm.
Closed for Monday lunches
ff

The house was converted into a pub in the 19th Century. It is a pleasant and friendly place with 6 bedrooms, a restaurant and a bar as well as a lounge. Children allowed indoors but dogs outside only.

C

Killoran Country House Hotel
Wetheral
☎ 01228 560 200
Last orders: 2.00pm and 9.00pm every day.
fff   Breakfasts

It was once owned by Rolls Royce. Since 1999 it has been a privately owned hotel with 9 bedrooms, restaurant, conservatory, bar and lounge, overlooking the River Eden with a view of Corby Castle on the other bank. Children are welcome inside but dogs in cars.

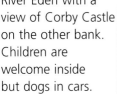

143

44	Carlisle
	Hawick Galashiels A7

The end of the M6 as a motorway, but it continues as the dual carriageway A74 over the Border where it becomes the A74(M). To get back from the Wallfoot Hotel (which is just five minutes) you will have to retrace your way back to Junction 44.

Places of interest
Hadrian's Wall.

 # Wallfoot Hotel & Restaurant
Crosby on Eden
☎ 01228 573 696
Last Orders: 2.00pm and 9.00pm No lunches on Mondays and Tuesdays. Breakfast.
££ 🛏

A small privately owned hotel with 7 bedrooms, a comfortable restaurant and a bar where lounge meals are served. Dogs and children permitted in the garden at rear. Breakfast for the passing motorist.

44	Carlisle
	Hawick Galashiels A7

B

Metal Bridge Inn

Blackford
☎ 01228 674 044
Last orders: 2.00pm and 9.00pm.
ff 🛏

An old coaching inn, four miles beyond
Junction 44, by the A74 on the banks of the
River Esk just before the Scottish Border. It is
privately owned and in addition to a restaurant
and small bar it has 5 bedrooms. It prides itself
on the Steak Pie which can be eaten outside
when admiring the view over the river to the
Solway Firth and the mountains of
Dumfriesshire beyond. Children and dogs
welcome, as are the many fishermen who
come here to stay.

CARLISLE

M6

NEWCASTLE
UPON-TYNE

A1(M)

LEEDS

• YORK

M1

M62

• HULL

M55

M65

M62

M181

M180

M6

M58

M61

MANCHESTER

M18

LIVERPOOL

M57

M62

M67

A1(M)

M63

M56

M60

SHEFFIELD

CHESTER

M6

M1

SHREWSBURY •

M54

M6 TOLL

M42

• PETERBOROUGH

M69

BIRMINGHAM

M6

A1(M)

M42

COVENTRY

M45

• CAMBRIDGE

M11

M50

M40

A1(M)

M5

M1

SWANSEA •

M4

M48

M25

M4

LONDON

CARDIFF

M2

BRISTOL

M3

M5

M25

M23

M26

M20

F01

SOUTHAMPTON

M27

A3(M)

• EXETER

M11

London to Cambridge

For those travelling to or from the south and the Channel Tunnel it is a good alternative to the M1 as it links the M25 with the A1(M) at Huntingdon.

The southern section goes past the newish town of Harlow and the congestion around Stansted Airport.

Once north of them, the countryside is pleasant enough and passes some attractive towns such as Saffron Walden and the imposing pile of Audley End. At Duxford is the American Air Museum. Cambridge of course is a must for anyone who has never been there.

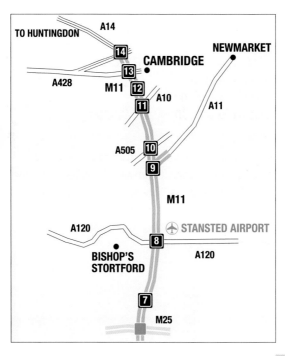

7 · Harlow A414 · Chelmsford

The roundabout is controlled by lights. Take the Chelmsford road and almost immediately turn off to the left on a small road which is marked St Clare Hospice and Hastingwood.

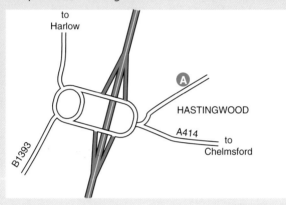

A The Rainbow and Dove

Hastingwood
☎ 01279 415 419
Last orders: 2.30pm and 9.30pm.
££

Said to date from the 15th century, it was a pub by 1640 when Cromwell's soldiers stopped to slake their thirst. There is outside seating in a garden and inside a roaring fire during the winter. Children discouraged, but dogs allowed in the grounds.

8 Stansted Airport
Bishop's Stortford A120

This junction is being modernised to cope with the increasing traffic to and from Stansted Airport requiring construction work. Keep going round the roundabout until you see the small turnoff for Birchanger.

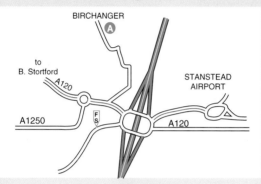

Ⓐ The Three Willows
Birchanger
☎ 01279 815 913
Last orders: 2.30pm and 9.30pm.
No evening meals on Sundays.
££

A quiet country pub with an interest in cricket, judging by the sign. Bar meals specialising in fish. Children's playground, where they are encouraged to stay. No dogs.

9 Newmarket A11
Norwich (Restricted access)

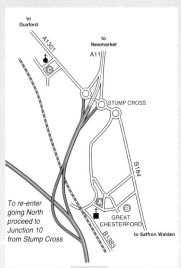

This junction gives direct access to the Newmarket road. Turn off where marked Great Chesterford before crossing over the road. If driving north, you must access again at Junction 10 and vice versa.

Places of interest

Audley End (EH), Saffron Walden

 A

The Crown House Hotel

Great Chesterford

☎ 01799 530 515

Last orders: 9.00pm including Sundays.

£££

There has been a building on the site since Roman times. The foundations of the present one date from 1560. It is a privately owned hotel with modern stone flagged floors and 22 bedrooms. Dogs and children are provided for.

9 | Newmarket A11
Norwich (Restricted access)

B ## The Plough
Great Chesterford
☎ 01799 530 283
Last orders: 2.20pm and 9.00pm.
No food on Sunday evenings.
££

A village pub for 200 years and owned by
Greene King. It has a modern restaurant and
bar. Large children's playground
and family room.
Outside seating
where children
and dogs
are welcome.

B ## The Red Lion
Hinxton
☎ 01799 530 601
Last orders: 1.45pm and 9.45pm
including Sundays.
£££

A 16th century pub in this attractive
village. Home cooking in the restaurant
and bar. The yellow headed Amazon
parrot is semi-retired, but a black cat,
Charlie, entertains the guests as
well as a stuffed tarantula.
Dogs and children
permitted in the
garden but
no coaches.

10 Royston A505 Newmarket A11

An easy enough junction but it could get congested when there is a flying display at the Imperial War Museum. Exit here if you are driving south to go to Great Chesterford or Saffron Walden.

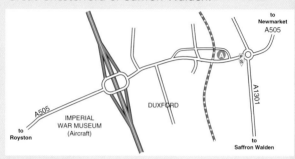

Places of interest
The Imperial War Museum
and American Air Museum.

 # The Red Lion Hotel
Whittlesford
☎ 01223 832 047
Last orders: 2.30pm and 9.00pm. Breakfast.
££ 🛏 Breakfast

An old black and white half timbered house, it is now a privately owned hotel with 17 bedrooms. The restaurant specialises in Greek omelettes and the bar serves snacks. Outside there is a large garden where children can play and dogs are allowed.
Breakfasts for the
passer by.

11 Royston A10

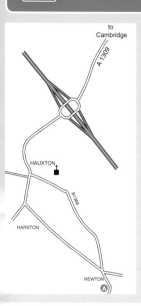

From the junction take the A10 to Royston. After about half a mile turn left onto the B1368 to Newton. The Queen's Head is on the other side of the village green

Places of interest
Docrwa's Manor
Willers Mill

 Queens Head
Newton
☎ 01223 870 436
Last orders: 2.30pm and 9.30pm every day.
£££

Pleasant and friendly with well furnished dining alcoves and bars and a host of interesting momentos. It is one of the dying breed of the traditional English pub. Children welcome and dogs outside.

12	Cambridge A603 Sandy

Do not be too put off by the modern development into Barton. The picturesque village of Grantchester is easy to find, which was made famous by the First World War poet Rupert Brooke, "....Is there honey still for tea?"

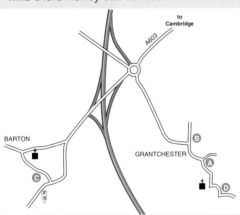

Places of interest
Wimpole Hall (NT)

Ⓐ **The Green Man**
Grantchester
☎ 01223 841 178
Last orders: 3.00pm and 9.00pm.
££

A pub in the centre of the village with wooden floors, a restaurant and a bar. Extensive car park at the rear.
Children and dogs allowed in the garden.
A comfort stop.

12	Cambridge A603 Sandy

B The Rupert Brooke

Grantchester

☎ 01223 840 295

Last orders: 2.30pm and 9.30pm.

£££

Converted from a 19th century house, into a folksy, but cheerful privately owned pub, complete with beams. There is outside seating at the front. and a patio and garden at the rear, overlooking the meadows. Children over 14 but no dogs or coaches.

C The White Horse

Barton

☎ 01223 262 327

Last orders: 2.00pm and 9.30pm.

££

A popular pub, owned by Greene King, which has recently been extended. It has a restaurant, carvery and a bar, as well as five bedrooms. Outside there is a beer garden and a car park. Children and dogs, but outside.

12	Cambridge A603 Sandy

 D

The Orchard

Grantchester

☎ 01223 845 788

Last orders: 10.30pm to 6.30pm.

£££　　✳

Now over 100 years old it is still an old fashioned tearooms complete with 1920s deckchairs, punts and nostalgia. You almost expect to see previous visitors such as Rupert Brooke, Virgina Woolf, A.A. Milne or John Betjeman appear from behind an apple tree. There are light lunches available as well as traditional teas indoors and out depending on the weather. Children and well trained dogs are welcome.

London to Cambridge

> **13/14** Cambridge A1303
> Bedford A428

Junction 13 is easy for those coming from the south, but Junction 14, for those from the North will require a Degree in map reading. However well worth the effort to get to Madingley.

Places of interest

◄ Madingley Hall.
◄ American Military Cemetary

The Three Horseshoes
Madingley
☎ 01954 210 221
Last orders: 2.00pm and 9.00pm.
On Sunday evenings Bar Grills are available.
££££ *

Part of a small group of well managed pub/restaurants run by chefs. It is efficient and smart. Inside there is a restaurant and long bar, with a conservatory at the rear. Outside there is a pleasant garden. A comfortable stop over.

M18

Rotherham to Goole

1 to **6**

This 30 mile motorway was built to link the M1 to the A1(M) at Doncaster, then with the M180 spur to Grimsby and finally with the M62 Trans Pennine near Goole. It is a useful linking motorway, as you can switch from the M1 or else cut off a corner when travelling from or to Hull. That being said the countryside is flat and uninteresting.

Selby however to the north of the intersection with the M62 is worth a visit, as the abbey was built at the same time and probably by the same masons as Durham Cathedral.

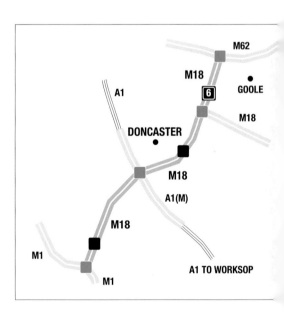

6   Thorne A614

This is an area of low fen land and irrigation ditches. The Waterside, where canal boats once disgorged their cargoes, was renowned for having seven pubs but only one now remains. It is said that an Elizabethan warship was built here to harass the Armada.

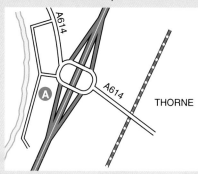

Places of interest
The birthplace of Thomas Crapper, the manufacturer of flushing lavatories.

The John Bull Inn
Waterside
☎ 01405 814 677
Last orders: 2.30pm and 9.30pm.
££

A traditional inn, by the canal, where ale has been served to thirsty bargemen since the 1500s. It has a restaurant which is used in the evening but otherwise serves bar meals. Children and dogs are welcome.

M20

London to Folkestone

1 to **13**

The M20 is 40 miles long and was started in 1961 and finished twenty years later. It is the main motorway from the Channel Ports to link up directly with the M25 and the motorway system.

It goes through some very attractive scenery, being the Garden of Kent and it should be enjoyed before it is engulfed with proposals to submerge it with new houses around Ashford. After Maidstone with its orchards and oast houses, the M20 climbs the shoulder of the North Weald on its way to London, whilst the M26 spur continues and links up with the southern segment of the M25.

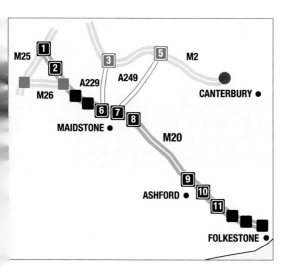

1 Junction with Exit 3 of the M25

It is not so complicated as it may appear. For those driving on the M20 follow the signs off for the M25. Those using the M25 follow the signs for the M20. On the roundabout it will be signed Farningham A20. Do not be put off by passing the Highways Recycling Centre. Turn right at the roundabout by the filling station. It is still a surprisingly attractive rural village although so near to London.

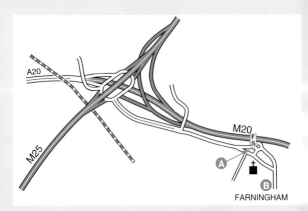

Places of interest
Eynsford Castle.(EH)
Lullingstone Roman Villa (EH).

London to Folkestone

| 1 | Junction with Exit 3 of the M25 |

Ⓐ
The Chequers
Farningham
☎ 01322 865 222
Last orders: 2.30pm.
£

A local pub serving bar meals at lunch only
with home made pies, sandwiches and a range
of beers and stout. Some
seating outside
on the pavement
and dogs are
welcome.
Street parking
only.

Ⓐ
Pied Bull
Farningham
☎ 01322 862 125
Last orders: 2.00pm and 8.45pm No evening
meals on Sundays. Closed Mondays.
££

It was known as The Bull in 1612. It has
recently been fully modernised and
produces bar meals, especially Steak
and Kidney pies.
Dogs and children
under control
welcomed in the
enclosed garden.

2   Paddock Wood Gravesend Tonbridge (A22)

Junction 2 is in reality two exits joined by a normal road. Coming from London it is easy enough to get off at the first exit to get to Wrotham, which is a picturesque village. You must then rejoin by driving to Junction 2a on the M26 which joins the M20 a mile further on! It is not as bad as it sounds. The converse is true for those driving from the Channel Tunnel.

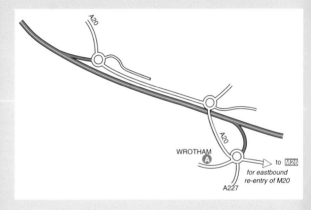

Places of interest
Brands Hatch Racing Circuit.

2 Paddock Wood Gravesend
Tonbridge (A22)

Bull Hotel
Wrotham
☎ 01732 789 800
Last orders: 2.00pm and 9.45pm
9.30pm on Sundays.
£££ 🛏

A family run hotel in a building which is a
listed Georgian house, but the interior has
been done over to give a modern open plan
dining area and bar. Morning coffee for the
passing motorist. For the overnight guests
there are 12 bedrooms.
A comfort stop.

6   Maidstone   Chatham A229

There have been road improvements to the A229
which has made it easier to reach the two places
mentioned.

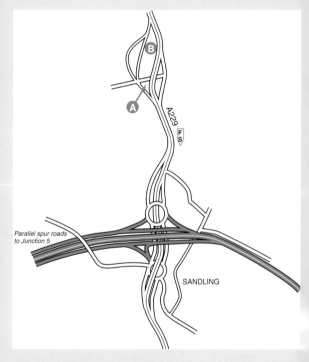

Places of interest
Kits Coty,
prehistoric burial mound
Museum of Kent life.

6 Maidstone Chatham A229

Ⓐ Lower Bell.
Blue Bell Hill
☎ 01634 861 127
Last orders: 2.45pm and 9.45pm.
££

The word Lower in the name is appropriate as it is now surrounded by high embankments of the new road layout. These do not detract from the warm welcome and choice of four Real Ales on offer.
There is some
outside seating
at the rear where
dogs are allowed.

Ⓑ Kits Coty Brasserie
Kits Coty
☎ 01634 684 445
Last orders: 2.00pm and 10.00pm.
Closed Saturday and Sunday evenings.
££

A family run restaurant and brasserie for the past sixteen years. It has sweeping views south over Maidstone and the Weald. A well kept garden enhances its surroundings. Modern art deco furnishing with glass and chrome.

Maidstone   Sheerness
Canterbury   Ramsgate A249

This junction is close to Maidstone and therefore it is a more built up area. The new Eurostar railtrack makes it more confusing.

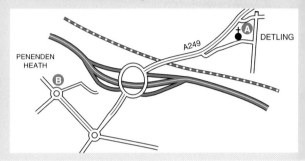

 The Cock Horse
Detling
☎ 01622 737 092
Last orders: From 11.00am to 10.30pm.
££

A local pub in the middle of this rural village although hemmed in by new roads. It has a beamed restaurant and bar, where imaginative home cooking is served and coffee all day. A secluded garden at the rear where dogs and children are welcome.

Maidstone   Sheerness
Canterbury   Ramsgate A249

The Chiltern Hundreds
Penenden Heath
☎ 01622 752 335
Last orders: 10.00pm. 9.30pm on Sundays.
£££

It has been a coaching stop since 1830. Why it should give the impression of giving an MP the chance to leave Parliament in a hurry is not known. It is part of the Chef and Brewer chain, so now has open areas serving bar meals from 11am. Some outside seating and a large carpark. Facilities for the disabled. Dogs not welcome. A comfort stop.

8   Lenham A20

Not a complicated junction but look out for the sign to Hollingbourne

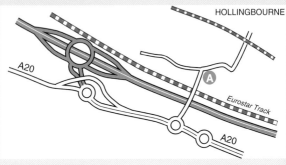

Places of interest

Leeds Castle. (HHA) Stoneacre. (NT)

Ⓐ The Windmill
Hollingbourne
☎ 01622 880 280
Last orders: 2.30pm and 10.00pm.
9.30pm on Sundays.
££ *

A privately owned pub, which dates back in parts to the 16th Century, in this attractive village. It has a restaurant and bar with home cooked meals. Outside there is a new playground and a beer garden at the rear, with seating in front. The resident dog takes priority over all canine visitors so check beforehand.

9 Ashford A20
Canterbury A28

A modern junction and road system, which does not seem to bode well in finding anything suitable, but persist.

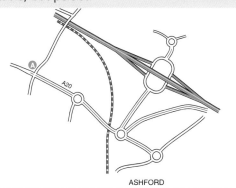

ASHFORD

Places of interest
Godington Park.

Hare and Hounds
Potters Corner
☎ 01233 621 760
Last orders: 2.30pm and 9.30pm.
Closed Monday evenings.
££

Once an 18th century inn, it has been thoroughly modernised, but still retains character and serves Real Ales. The road outside is busy but there is some outside seating.

10　Ashford A292

A built up area, not helped by a large Tesco just off the Motorway. The pubs is pleasant enough when you reach it but you may prefer to treat it as comfort stops.

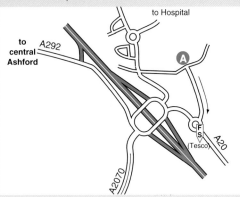

Ⓐ Blacksmiths Arms

Willesborough Green
☎ 01233 623 975
Last orders: 2.30pm and 9.00pm.
9.00pm on Sundays.
££

Some 300 years old and probably the old smithy, the forge is now replaced by log fires and the heat reduced by pints of Real Ale, in either the beamed restaurant or the bar.
There is a large garden at the
rear where dogs
are welcome.
One Armed Bandits
for the bored.

> **11** Canterbury B 2068
> Hastings A259   Hythe A261

The new Eurostar track now runs alongside the
motorway. Circle round to the north on the B
2068 and the pub can be seen on the left.

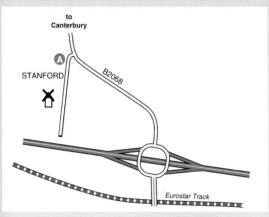

A The Drum
Stanford
☎ 01303 812 125
Last orders: 2.30pm and 9.00pm.
££

It is the last pub before (or first after) the
Tunnel. It has been a country pub for some
200 years. Log fires still burn in the grates.
There is a restaurant and a bar for snacks
and Real Ales. Outside seating in the
garden. Dogs welcome. Sunday Roasts
are their speciality.

M23

Caterham to Crawley

7 to **11**

Built to give quick access from Gatwick Airport to London, this 18 mile stretch took nearly four years to complete. However, the roads south of Croydon are such that many motorists prefer to head west out of London to link up with the M25 and then drive round to the M23.

Gatwick Airport started life as a racecourse in the 19th century before becoming one of the busiest airports in the UK in spite of only having one runway.

At Junction 11 it continues as the A23 to Brighton.

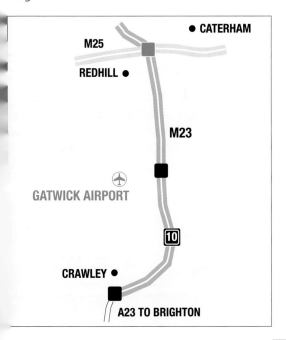

10	Crawley East Grinstead A264

An easy junction and the Hotel is on the other side of the roundabout.a

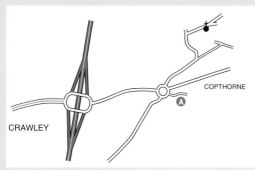

Places of interest
Wakehurst Place (NT)

 Copthorne Hotel
Copthorne
☎ 01342 714 971
Last orders: 2.00pm and 10.45pm.
ffff 🛏

It started life in the 16th century, but has grown out of all proportion since then. Today the White Swan is all that is left of that age and is now one of the bars. Elsewhere there are 227 bedrooms, full range of leisure activities and two restaurants. It is geared for the business community and conferences, but still has time to give a welcome to the passing motorist.

London Orbital

1a to **30**

The idea of an orbital ring road round London was first mooted in 1905. The North Circular Road was built in the 1930s but the South Circular exists in name only.

In 1975 a decision was made to construct an integrated Orbital Ring Road which was finally completed in 1986. It was originally intended to have more lanes but this was deemed to be too expensive. It will now cost a fortune to upgrade to cope with the increase in traffic.

The M25 does however make it easier for visitors from abroad to skirt around London and head north or west.

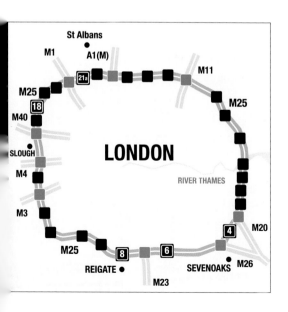

4   Bromley A21
Orpington A224

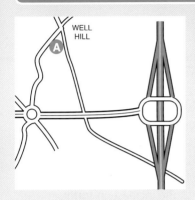

As a junction it is an easy one but at the roundabout look out for a narrow lane signed Well Hill.

Places of interest

Lullingstone
Roman VIlla (EH) Lullingstone Castle(HHA)
Eynsford Castle (EH).

 Bo Peep Restaurant
Well Hill
☎ 01959 534 457
Last orders: 2.00m and 9.45pm.
No evening meals on Sundays.
££   *

It has been an alehouse since 1549. It is a surprise to find it, so close to London, in the middle of strawberry fields.
It has a Non Smoking restaurant and a bar for snacks.
A well kept garden and inside, a friendly welcome.

London Orbital

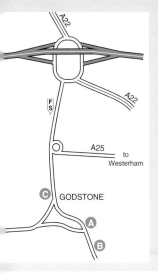

> **6** Westerham Eastbourne
> Caterham Godstone A22

This should not be any trouble but do not take the dual carriageway. Godstone is an attractive place, surrounding a village green.

Places of interest
Chartwell (NT)
Squerryes Court (HHA)
Quebec House.

Ⓐ The White Hart
Godstone
☎ 01883 742 521
Last orders: 2.30pm and 10.30pm
9pm on Sundays.
££

According to the blurb, it was established in the reign of Richard II and enlarged at the time of Good Queen Bess. It is now part of the Beefeater chain and therefore somewhat formalised. It is still a cheerful place with original beams, log fires and efficient service. There is outside seating and a car park.

179

6 Westerham Eastbourne
Caterham Godstone A22

B Coach House Restaurant and Godstone Hotel

Godstone

☎ 01883 742 461

Last orders: 2.00pm and 10.00pm.
9.00pm on Sundays

£££ 🛏

A comfortable friendly family run hotel. It is
some 400 years old, but apparently not as old
as the willow tree in the garden. For those
wishing to stay, after tasting one of their
flambéed specialities at dinner in the Coach
House Restaurant, there are 8 double
bedrooms available.
Dogs are welcome but outdoors.

London Orbital

6	Westerham Eastbourne Caterham Godstone A22

C The Hare and Hounds

Godstone

☎ 01883 742 296

Last orders: 3.00pm and 9.00pm.
9.00pm on Sundays.

ff

A traditional English village pub, with beamed eating areas. There is some outside seating under a spreading chestnut tree. Children and dogs are not encouraged, but inside there is a friendly welcome.

8 Sutton Reigate A217

Keep a look-out after the roundabout as you might easily miss the turning. If you do, carry on to the crossroads.

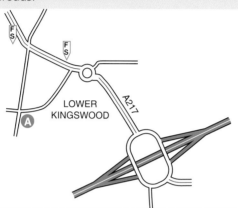

Ⓐ Mint Arms
Lower Kingswood
☎ 01737 242 957
Last orders: 3pm and 10.00pm.
9.30pm on Sundays.
£££

A Free House tucked away in a small village. It does have a restaurant as well as the usual bars for meals. Outside there is a playground, a beer garden where they have Barbecues, weather permitting and dogs and children are allowed. A pool table and dart board for wet days.

18 Rickmansworth Chorleywood

An easy junction but at the cross roads look out for Dog Kennel Road.

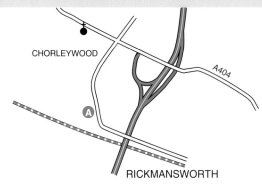

CHORLEYWOOD

A404

(A)

RICKMANSWORTH

Places of interest
Chenies Manor House.

(A) # The Black Horse
Chorleywood Common
☎ 01923 282 252
Last orders: 2.15pm and 9.15pm.
£££ *

This could be deep in the countryside instead of being just off the motorway. It has been a pub since the early 1800s and still produces home cooked specials. There is seating at the front and a beer garden at the rear. Children are welcome and dogs can stretch their legs on the Common.

21a St Albans A405

This looks a a complicated junction but you just follow the signs.

Places of interest
St Albans Abbey.
Verulanium Roman City.

Ⓐ Thistle St Albans

Chiswell Green
☎ 01727 854 252
Last orders: 2.00pm and 9.30pm.
9pm on Sundays.
££££ 🛏 Breakfast

This hotel is not for the casual passer-by, as it sets a high standard in comfort and price. There are 111 bedrooms to suit every wish and supported by every form of comfort and relaxation, such as a swimming pool, gym and a sauna. There is a restaurant, carvery and bars. Children and dogs are welcomed. Breakfast for passing motorists.

M20/M25 Link

2a Borough Green
Maidstone A25

An 8 mile stretch of motorway, built in 1980, to form a link from the M20 with the southern segment of the M25. Useful for those who have misread the M20 signs and find themselves on the M26 going west, as they can rejoin the M20 at Junction 2a to Wrotham.

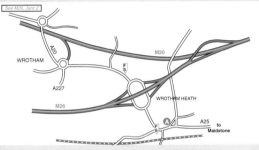

Places of interest
Old Soar Manor (EH) , Ightam Mote. (NT)
St Leonards Tower. (EH)

The Vineyard
Wrotham Heath
☎ 01732 882 330
Last orders: 2.30pm and 10.30pm.
£££

A family run restaurant, specialising in sea food and French and Italian cooking. Although on the road, it is surrounded by a secluded garden and private car park. Small and friendly. Children allowed but no dogs.

185

M27

New Forest to Portsmouth

1 to **12**

The M27, 27 miles long, was built to connect
Portsmouth and Southampton with the M3. It
starts or ends rather abruptly at the edge of
the New Forest, but continues as a dual
carriageway nearly as far as Bournemouth.
At the Portsmouth end it joins up with the
A3(M) before carrying on as a dual-carriageway
to Chichester, Brighton and Lewes (with some
breaks). It is conceivable that one day there
could be a motorway along the south coast to
Dover. This would help alleviate the plight of
foreign visitors who at present have to head
for London and the M25, whatever their
destination.

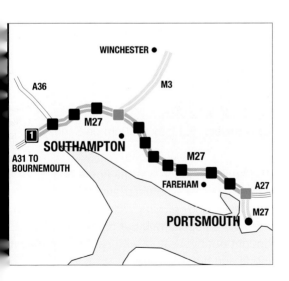

1   Lyndhurst
Cadnam A337

Once off the junction, you might miss the sign to
the Sir John Barleycorn on your left. To the north
of the junction, the road will take you into the
New Forest proper, but you will not get lost.

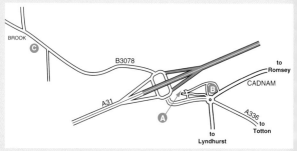

Places of interest
The Rufus Stone. Hamptworth Lodge (HHA)
Broadlands House (HHA) Paulton's Park.
Newhouse, Redlynch.(HHA)

A Sir John Barleycorn
Cadnam
☎ 02380 812 236
Last orders: 9.30pm. 9.00pm on Sundays.
££

The original cottage was the home of a
charcoal burner who discovered the newly
murdered body of King William Rufus in 1100.
It is now a popular pub but has recently been
bought out by Alcatraz who have refurbished it
inside and out. Dogs are
allowed in the
beer garden,
where .

1	Lyndhurst Cadnam A337

B The White Hart

Cadnam
☎ 02380 812 277
Last orders: 2pm and 9.30pm
9pm on Sundays.
£££   *

A Coaching Inn since the 17th century, it still gives warm hospitality with log fires and a profusion of hanging baskets.
Home cooking, specialising in fish.
There is a playground and a secluded garden where dogs are allowed.

C The Green Dragon

Brook
☎ 02380 813 359
Last orders: 2.00pm and 9.30pm.
9.00pm on Sundays.
£££

A Whitbred owned pub. It has been a Beerhouse for 200 years, before which it was used by a coffin maker and before him by a wheelwright. No sign of the coffin maker is now apparent, only a friendly, cheerful atmosphere in the large bar with beamed areas for eating.

M40

London to Birmingham

2 to **16**

The first section to Oxford was completed in 1976 but it took fifteen years to link it to the M42. It was completed in 1991 to take the pressure off the M1, to such an extent that now it is almost as crowded.

Beware of Junction 15 with five roads converging on the roundabout as at present it can take up to half an hour to reach the dual carriageway to Coventry. There is no police presence there but once on the dual carriageway, motorists trying to catch up on lost time could be caught for speeding.

Chesterton Windmill is a prominent landmark on the high ground to the east of the motorway, north of Junction12.

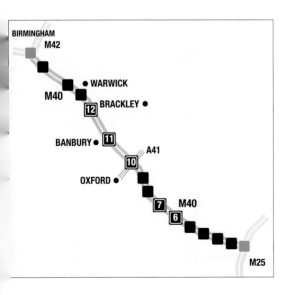

6   Watlington   Thame
Princes Risborough B4009

The road to Lewknor can be easily missed, so look out for the sign on the right. The village itself is attractive.

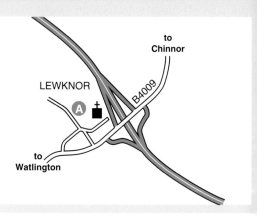

A Ye Olde Leather Bottel
Lewknor
☎ 01844 351 482
Last orders: 2.00pm and 9.30pm.
£££   *

Ye Olde Leather Bottel is 450 years old, which makes for a congenial and friendly atmosphere. It specialises in home cooking and serves morning coffee as well as Brakspears Traditional Ales. There is plenty of outside seating in a large garden. Dogs welcome.

7   Wallingford A379. Thame

Coming from London there is no difficulty in exiting but returning to the motorway you will have to cross over it, take the A40 and (A418) to Oxford and join up with the motorway at Junction 8A. Coming from the north take the A418 signed Aylesbury and Thame and then the A40 and the A379 to Wallingford. To continue on to London follow the signs at Junction 7.

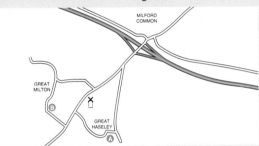

Places of interest Rycote Chapel

The Plough
Great Haseley
☎ 01844 279 283
Last orders: 2.00pm and 10.00pm every day
£££

A thatched roofed pub in the centre of a pleasant rural village. It has recently been taken over. Extensive remodelling will be taking place internally. Outside seating and gravel car park. Children and dogs are welcome.

7 Wallingford A379. Thame

Le Manoir aux Quat' Saisons

Great Milton

☎ 01844 278 881

Last orders: 2.30pm and 9.30pm.

£££££   🛏   Breakfast   ★

This must be the most famous restaurant in the country. It is in an old-fashioned setting with a large well kept garden. There are 32 bedrooms, three restaurant and a conservatory. Children but dogs outside. An experience in every sense of the word.

10 Northampton A43

A simple junction off the motorway on to the old road between Oxford and Brackley.

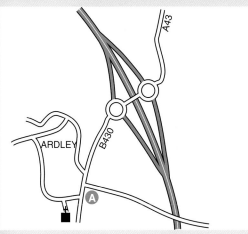

Fox and Hounds
Ardley
☎ 01869 346 883
Last orders: 2.15pm and 9.00pm.
Closed on Sunday evenings.
££

Now owned by an ex-mariner, this 18th Century pub serves traditional ales and a selection of bar meals. A beer garden at the rear with its own car parking. Children are welcome, as are ex-servicemen who served nearby.

11   Banbury A422

This is the junction for Banbury. Take the A422 to Brackley and after half a mile take the second left at the roundabout signed Middleton Cheney.

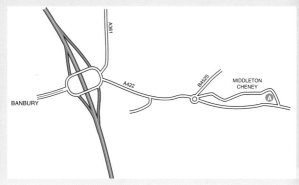

Ⓐ New Inn
Middleton Cheney
☎ 01295 719 399
Last orders: 2.00pm and 9.00pm.
No evening meals on Sundays
££

A tenanted pub of Bass, but it has a traditional and friendly atmosphere with flagstoned floors, serving bar meals. A beer garden where children and dogs are welcome.

12 Gaydon B4451

Turn left when you get to the A41 and the pub will be signed on your right hand side.

Places of interest

Heritage Motor Museum
Edgehill Battlefield.1642
Upton House (NT).

Ⓐ The Malt Shovel Inn
Gaydon
☎ 01926 641 221
Last orders: 2.00pm and 9.00pm.
seven days a week
£££

A deservedly popular village inn with a bar and a restaurant area. The owners who used to run auberges and hotels in France are proud of their claim of real food with real ale. Dogs and children are welcome provided they behave themselves.

NEWCASTLE
UPON-TYNE

CARLISLE

M6

A1(M)

LEEDS • YORK

M55 M65 •HULL
M6 M62 M62
M57 M58 M61 M181
LIVERPOOL MANCHESTER M18
M63 M56 M62 M67 M180
M60 A1(M)
CHESTER SHEFFIELD

SHREWSBURY • M54 M1

M6 •PETERBOROUGH

M6 TOLL
M42 A1(M)

BIRMINGHAM M69
M6
M42 COVENTRY •CAMBRIDGE
M45 M11
M40
M50 M1 A1(M)
M5 M25
M48 LONDON
SWANSEA• M4 M2
CARDIFF BRISTOL M4
M3 M25 M26 M20
M23 F0
M5 M27 A3(M)
SOUTHAMPTON
EXETER

M42

Bromsgrove to Tamworth

M42

2 to **11**

Completed in 1986, it is still to be continued as a motorway to join up with the M1 at Nottingham. It is in effect the southern part of the Birmingham Ring Road, with the M6 and the M5 completing the circuit. It is a useful linkage for those using the M40 from and to the north and also for those who are hoping to avoid the delays at Spaghetti Junction, by using the M5.

The opening of the M6(Toll) to the north will help reduce this problem

3 Birmingham   Redditch
Evesham A435

Take the slip road towards Portway – over the dual carriageway and back towards the restaurant.

(A) ## Portway Italian Restaurant
Portway
☎ 01564 824 794
Last orders: 2.30pm and 10.30pm.
No evening meals on Sunday. Closed Monday.
££

An Italian restaurant obviously specialising in Italian dishes. A comfortable small restaurant. No dogs.

11 Burton on Trent
Nuneaton A444

A twisty road
system to reach
Appleby Magna,
but not
impossible.
Keep the church
in view.a

Ⓐ The Black Horse

Appleby Magna
☎ 01530 270 588
Last orders: 9.30pm. No lunches on
weekdays.Bar lunches on Sundays but no
evening meals.
£

An old 16th or 17th Century building. It is
a simple village pub owned by Marstons.
It serves bar meals and has some outside
seating as well as a family room. Dogs are
welcome.

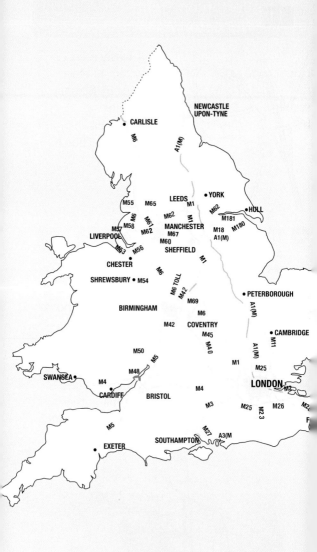

NEWCASTLE
UPON-TYNE

CARLISLE

M6

A1(M)

LEEDS ● YORK

M55 M65 M62 ● HULL

M6 M1

M58 M61 M62 M181

M62 MANCHESTER M18 M180

LIVERPOOL M57 M60 M67 A1(M)

M53 M56

CHESTER SHEFFIELD

SHREWSBURY ● M54 M6 M1

M6 TOLL

M42

BIRMINGHAM M69

M6

M42 COVENTRY

M45

M40

M50 ● PETERBOROUGH

M5 A1(M)

M48 ● CAMBRIDGE

SWANSEA ● M4 M11

CARDIFF M1

BRISTOL A1(M)

M4 M25

LONDON M2

M3

M25 M26 M2

M5 M23

M27 A3(M)

SOUTHAMPTON

EXETER ●

M48 (ex M4)

Aust to Chepstow

1 Avonmouth A403

This used to be the last junction on the M4 before crossing over into Wales. With the building of another bridge over the Severn, this section was renamed M48 and the new section became the M4, for some illogical reason.

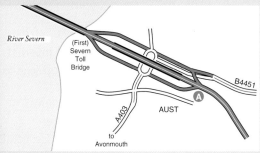

Places of interest
St Augustine's Vineyard

Ⓐ **Boars Head**
Aust
☎ 01454 632 278
Last orders: 2.15pm and 9.15pm.
No evening meals on Sundays.
£££

A late 18th Century pub which probably was a coaching stop for those crossing over to Wales on the ferry. It gives a friendly welcome to all, enhanced in winter by log fires and home made cooking.
There is a beer garden where dogs are welcome.

2　Chepstow A48

Chepstow, just off the junction, is well worth a visit especially the castle. There are other restaurants, hotels and pubs in the town.

Places of interest
Tintern Abbey. (EH)
Caerwent
(Roman Silures)
Offa's Dyke.
Chepstow Castle. (EH

 Wye Knot
Cheptstow
☎ 01291 622 929
Last orders: 2.00pm and 10.00pm. Closed Sunday evening and all day Monday.
£££

A privately owned restaurant on the banks of the River Wye with a varied menu cooked by two award winning chefs. A plaque on the wall outside says that the Chartists sailed from here in 1840 for Tasmania. Well-behaved children welcome but dogs outside.
Booking advisable.

| 2 | Chepstow A48 |

 B

Castle View Hotel
Chepstow
☎ 01291 620 349
Last orders: 2.00pm and 9.30pm.
Residents only for Sunday evenings.
£££   🛏

As the name implies, it really does have a view up to the castle. Some 350 years old, it has been modernised to provide 13 bedrooms mostly in external annexes. Outside there is a beer garden at the rear, whilst indoors there is a restaurant and a bar. There are facilities for the disabled. Children and dogs are welcome.

NEWCASTLE UPON-TYNE

CARLISLE

M6

A1(M)

LEEDS • YORK

M55 M65 M1

M62

M6 HULL

M58 M61 M62 M1 M181

M57 M62 M18 M180

LIVERPOOL M56 M67 A1(M)

M53 M56 M60

SHEFFIELD

CHESTER

M6 M1

SHREWSBURY • M54

M6 TOLL

M4.2

BIRMINGHAM M69

M6

M42 COVENTRY

M45

M40

M50 A1(M)

PETERBOROUGH

CAMBRIDGE

M11

M5

M1 M25

SWANSEA • M48

M4 LONDON M2

CARDIFF

BRISTOL M4 M25 M23 M26

M3

M5

M27 A3(M

EXETER SOUTHAMPTON

M50

M5 to Ross on Wye

1 to 4

The M50 was one of the first motorways to be built and for some years was in splendid isolation until joined to the M 5. It was built to connect the Midlands with South Wales but only goes as far as Ross on Wye before continuing as dual-carriageway to Newport. It is also a way of driving to Wales without paying the Toll charges levied on the Severn Bridges!

There are a wealth of places to see, not too far from the motorway. Ross on Wye is a market town with interesting old buildings. Nearby is the picturesque Symons Yat where the river Wye winds through a gorge below the imposing ruins of Goodrich Castle.
To the south of Ross is the Forest of Dean famous amongst other things for the small family coal mines still in private ownership.
To the west is the town of Monmouth with its medieval bridge and further on the ruins of Raglan Castle destroyed by Cromwell.

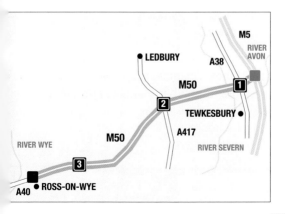

1 Malvern   Tewkesbury A38

A relatively easy junction. Just follow the signs to
Twyning. The Fleet Inn is brown signed from the
roundabout.

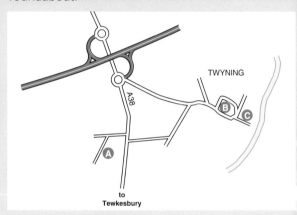

Places of interest
Tewkesbury Abbey.

 Puckrup Hall Hotel
Puckrup
☎ 01684 296 200
Last orders: 2.00pm and 10.00pm but
food available 24 hours.
££££   🛏

A Hilton Hotel with all the facilities including
an 18 hole Championship Golf Course, two
restaurants and bars, leisure centre and
swimming pool. It has
112 bedrooms
(16 in the original
building).

1 Malvern Tewkesbury A38

B The Village Inn
Twyning
☎ 01684 293 500
Last orders: 2.30pm and 11.00pm.
Closed Mondays and Tuesdays lunch.
£

Overlooking the village green, it was
once a bakery, then a shop and
Post office and is now a
friendly old
fashioned pub.

B The Fleet Inn
Twyning
☎ 01684 274 310
Last orders: 9.00pm. in the restaurant.
££ 🛏

By the side of the River Avon, it is a popular
place, with some bedrooms.
An open area for bar meals
and outside seating on
a terrace by the
banks of the river.
Dogs allowed
on leads.

Gloucester A417
Hereford   Ledbury 417

Take the road to Gloucester to find the Rose and
Crown which is about a mile from the junction

Places of interest
Eastnor Castle. (HHA)

 The Rose and Crown
Redmarly D'Abitot
☎ 01531 650 234
Last orders: 2.00pm and 9.15pm
No evening meals on Sundays.
££

A wayside pub dating from the 1800s with the
addition of a later Assembly Room which is
now the restaurant. Now owned by
Pubmasters, it has a bar and outside
seating. Dogs
and children
allowed.
A comfort stop.

3 Newent B4221

The only T junction exit in the U.K which is known in the trade as a Compact Grade Separation! Take the road to Kilcot.

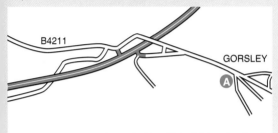

The Roadmaker Inn
Gorsley
☎ 01989 720 352
Last orders: 2.00pm and 9.00pm
No food on Sunday & Monday nights.
££

A Free House, specialising in local beef and vegetables. Children but no dogs. Outside seating and a congenial atmosphere as it has been a pub since 1840.

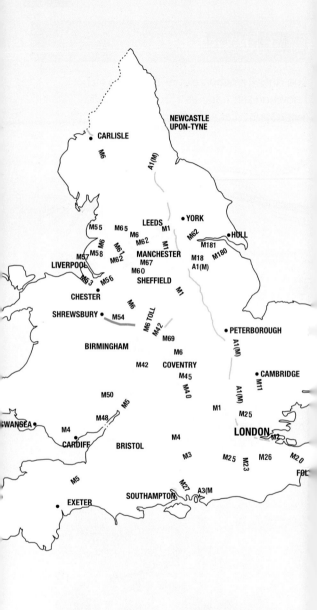

M53

Birkenhead to Chester

1 to **12**

This short 12 mile stretch of motorway is interesting as it passes through the densely industrialised area of Ellesmere Port as well as some pleasant wooded countryside. Port Sunlight is the home of margerine and the Leverhulme's amazing house and art collection. There are apparently more millionaires in the Wirral than elsewhere in the UK excluding the London area.

At the other end of the motorway is Chester, still a walled city with medieval buildings and once the home base of the Roman XX (Victrix) Legion.

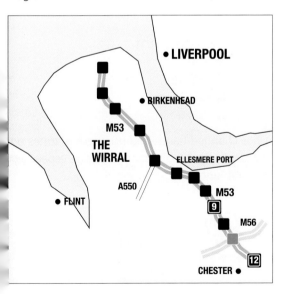

> **9**   Ellesmere Port
> Boat Museum A50532

Just follow the signs to the Boat Museum, which is well worth a visit.

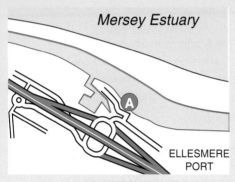

Mersey Estuary

ELLESMERE
PORT

Places of interest
The Boat Museum.

Ⓐ Rotate Restaurant
Ellesmere Port
☎ 01513 551 163
Last orders: 9.30pm.
£

It has changed hands and now concentrates on contemporary Mediterranean cuisine especially for light lunches.

Birkenhead to Chester

12   Chester A51

There is a danger of continuing past the junction onto the dual carriageway A55 to Wales.

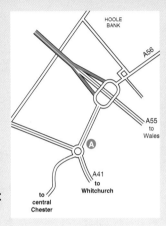

HOOLE BANK

A56

A55
to
Wales

Ⓐ

A41
to
Whitchurch

to
central
Chester

Places of interest
Chester.

Ⓐ Hoole Hall Hotel
Chester
☎ 01244 350 011
Last orders: 2.00pm and 9.15pm.
£££   🛏   Breakfast

In 1785, it was the home of the pioneer balloonist the Reverand Thomas Baldwin. In the last war it was occupied by the Army and remained derelict for many years. It was rebuilt in 1990 as a hotel set in five acres of garden, 97 bedrooms and a conference centre. For passing motorists bar meals are available in the lounge bar and an excellent breakfast in the conservatory.

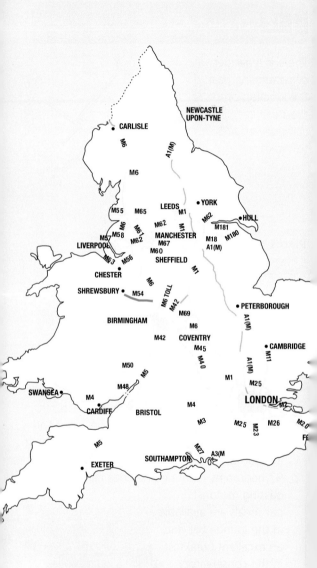

M54

Wolverhapton to Telford

1 to **7**

A 23 mile stretch of motorway which was opened in 1975 to link Birmingham to Shrewsbury and Wales. Beyond Telford it has been upgraded to a modern dual carriageway to the other side of Shrewsbury.

After coming off the M6 it passes through pleasant farming countryside until the much vaunted Telford New Town, which is typical of 1960s planning - interminable tree lined roads and roundabouts with sparse signing.

The countryside around is well worth a visit. Bridgnorth, reduced by Cromwell; the Ironbridge Gorge, the cradle of modern industry and medieval Much Wenlock with its Priory. To the west of Telford rises the Wrekin, acting as the gateway to the Welsh Border and close by, the ruins of the Roman administrative town of Wroxeter with its massive public baths. Shrewsbury itself is one of the most attractive county towns in England with a wealth of old buildings.

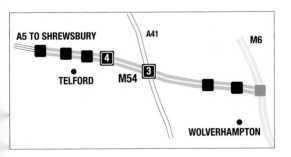

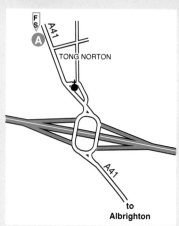

A rural part of Shropshire. The Bell Inn is almost too easy to find as you can drive past it. Look out for the Murco Filling Station.

Places of interest Weston Park. (HHA) Boscobel House and the Royal Oak Tree. Aerospace Museum. Lillieshall Abbey.

 Bell Inn
Tong
☎ 01952 851 210
Last orders: 9.00pm on Sundays to Wednesdays.10.00pm Thursdays to Saturdays.
£

An old coaching inn from the 18th century, with interesting stables. Modernised by Bank's Brewery, it has a restaurant, non smoking bars and a conservatory. Behind there is a beer garden and a playground. Children and dogs are welcome.
There are facilities for the disabled.
A comfort stop.

4 Bridgnorth A442

Get off the M54 at Junction 4 and take the A442 to Bridgnorth, winding around several roundabouts and with endless avenues leading off in different directions. Norton is about 8 miles south

Ⓐ Hundred House Hotel
Norton
☎ 01952 730 353
Last orders: 2.00pm and 9.30pm every day.
£££ 🛏 Breakfast

It was once courthouse and the stocks are still in place on the other side of the road. It is now a friendly family hotel with10 bedrooms, two dining areas and a bar. Children and dog are welcome provided they behave themselves

M56

Manchester to Chester

1 to **16**

Some 37 miles long, it connects Manchester with the commuter areas in Cheshire as well as Chester and North Wales beyond. It is not particularly attractive especially when coming out of Manchester and past the Airport. However once over the intersection with the M6 (a complicated junction, badly signed) it gets slightly better. At the end of the motorway it continues into Wales as a dual carriageway.

On a clear day Beeston Castle can be seen to the south on a bluff of high ground, after passing Frodsham. The historic city of Chester was once the base of the Roman XX (Victrix) Legion. It still has its medieval walls and was where the architect Sir John Vanbrugh grew up.

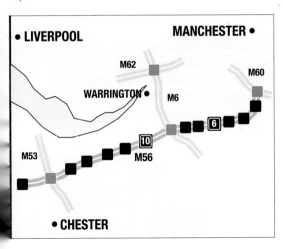

6   Wilmslow   Macclesfield   Hale   A538

A certain amount of skill is required to negotiate the roundabouts and you may miss the turn off down Sunbank Lane.

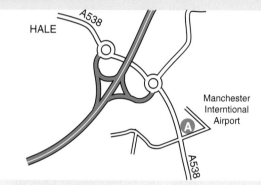

Ⓐ The Romper
Hale Barns
☎ 01619 806 806
Last orders: 11,00pm. 10.30pm on Sundays.
££

Owned now by Scottish and Newcastle it was once an old fashioned pub in a backwater but has been enlarged and well modernised, complete with dried hops. There is a beer garden and a large car park. Dogs are welcome outside as well as children.

> **10** Northwich Warrington
> A559

The Birch and Bottle seems to be further than one expects, but keep on. There are some new purpose built Road Houses as well, visible from the junction.

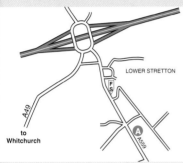

Places of interest
Anderton Boat Lift (EH) Arley Hall. (HHA)

Ⓐ Birch and Bottle
Lower Stretton
☎ 01925 730 225
Last orders: 3.00pm and 11.00pm.
10.30 on Sundays.
££

Owned by Greenalls, it is a cheerful place with a restaurant in the conservatory, where you can enjoy their speciality (Black Pudding). This could date from the time when it was built in 1814 as a wayside pub.
There is a beer garden for the hardy and his dog.

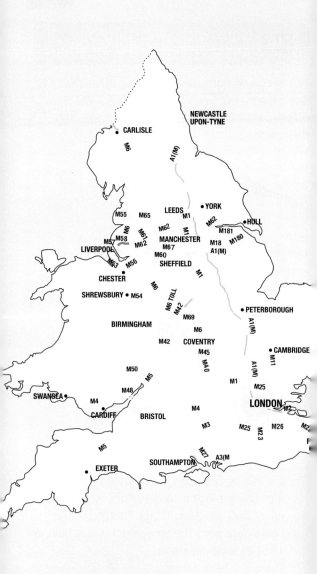

NEWCASTLE
UPON-TYNE

CARLISLE

M6

A1(M)

LEEDS
M1
YORK
M62
HULL
M55
M65
M62
M181
M6
M58
M1
M180
M57
M62
MANCHESTER
M18
LIVERPOOL
M67
A1(M)
M63
M60
M56
SHEFFIELD
CHESTER
M1
SHREWSBURY • M54
M6
M6 TOLL
PETERBOROUGH
M42
A1(M)
M69
BIRMINGHAM
M6
COVENTRY
CAMBRIDGE
M42
M45
M11
M50
M40
M5
A1(M)
M48
M1
SWANSEA •
M4
M25
CARDIFF
BRISTOL
LONDON
M4
M2
M3
M25
M26
M5
M2 3
M27
A3(M)
SOUTHAMPTON
EXETER

M58

Liverpool to Wigan

1 to **5**

Not the most exciting motorway, but it fulfills a useful function of linking Liverpool with the M6 by Wigan. It starts near the Aintree Racecourse, the venue for the Grand National, where it intersects with the M57, which is the western section of a non existant ring road around Liverpool.

It would be nice to be able to rattle off a list of places to visit off the motorway to reduce the tedium but that is not possible. The best hope is to look forward to lunch or dinner or else to drive into Wigan, long the butt of Music Hall humour but curiously enough not nearly so bad as its reputation.

Liverpool itself must be worth a visit if only to see the Tate of the North in their new home in the Docks, which is a magnificent example of what can be done with imagination and foresight.

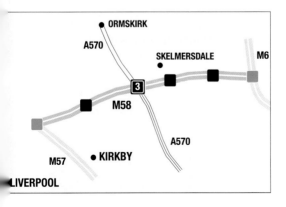

3   St. Helens   Ormskirk A570

You might miss the Quattro Restaurant, which is on what looks like a layby to the left as soon as you get off the roundabout.

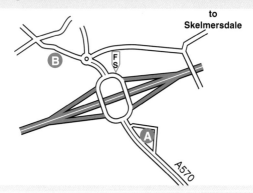

Ⓐ Quattro
Bickerstaffe
☎ 01695 720 800
Last orders: 2.00pm and 10.30pm.
Closed Mondays and Saturdays for lunch.
£££

As the name implies, it is an Italian restaurant with the usual cheerful atmosphere. It relies on its food, rather than beer gardens and the like, to attract customers of which some fifty can lunch or dine at the same time.
Children and dogs are welcome.

3 St. Helens   Ormskirk A570

The Sandpiper
Bickerstaffe
☎ 01695 733 666
Last orders: 10.00pm. 9.30pm on Sundays.
££

Once a farmhouse, it is now one of the
modern generation of purpose designed pubs
with outside seating in a garden and a large
carpark. It has a friendly atmosphere and
welcomes dogs outdoors. Bar meals served all
day in an open space bar area where you can
still smoke.

Parts of the ringroad had been known in the past as the M63 and the M62, as well as the M66. It has now been renumbered after the completion of the entire Orbital Motorway as the M60 and the old junction numbers have also been changed. Even the section of the M62, which bypassed Manchester to the north, is numbered M60. The M67 to the east had nothing that we could find. Even the M66 with such names as Ramsbottom was a disappointment. It would be best to hurry round Manchester, as the only place which gives hint of a comfort stop would be Jacksons Boat at Sale.

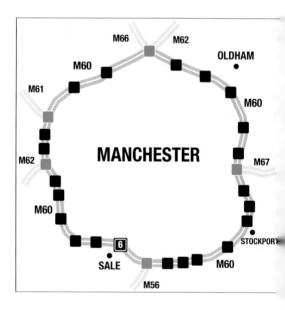

6 (ex 8) Sale A144

The access to Jacksons Boat is down a narrow country lane past a golf course to the right.

Jacksons Boat
Sale
☎ 0161 973 8549
Last call: 11.00pm
£

This must once have been frequented by bargees plying their trade on the River Mersey. At present it has been impossible for the management to find a chef, so for the time being no food is being served. There is a playground and a large beer garden where both dogs and children can stretch their legs.

NEWCASTLE
UPON-TYNE

CARLISLE

M6

A1(M)

LEEDS   • YORK

M55   M65   M1   M62   HULL
M6   M62   M181
M57 M58   M62   M11   M18   M180
LIVERPOOL   M62   MANCHESTER   A1(M)
M53   M56   M67
CHESTER   M60
SHEFFIELD
SHREWSBURY • M54   M6
M1
M6 TOLL
M42   M69
BIRMINGHAM   M6
M42   COVENTRY   • PETERBOROUGH
M45   A1(M)
M40   • CAMBRIDGE
M50   A1(M)   M11
M5   M1
M48   M25
SWANSEA •   M4   M25
CARDIFF   M4   LONDON   M2
BRISTOL   M3   M25   M26   M20
M5   M23
EXETER   M27   A3(M)
SOUTHAMPTON

M61

Manchester to Preston

M61

1 to **9**

A useful motorway for those living in and around Manchester who are going to or coming from the Lake District or the north. It is also an alternative for motorists driving over the Pennines on the M62 to connect with the M1 or the M6. Apart from that there is little that can be said for it.

About the only redeeming feature is the sight of the Pennines to the east looming over the outer suburbs of Manchester and Bolton. The place names such as Whittle le Woods or Bottom o' th' Moor have a certain charm.

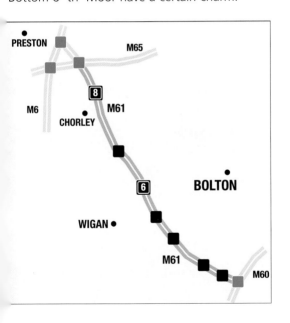

6 Chorley   Horwich A6027
Bolton

An uninteresting junction, but the view across to the Pennines over the Reebok Football Stadium is good.

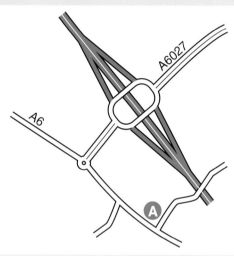

Ⓐ Royal Oak

West Houghton

☎ 01942 812 168

Last orders: 10.00pm.

££

A wayside stop since the 1830s, it is now part of a group and has been modernised to serve home cooked bar meals all day.
A comfort stop.

> **8** Blackburn   Leyland
> Southport A6

The Red Cat requires concentration as you have to drive past it and then come round behind it.

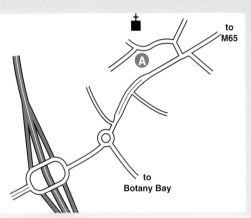

Ⓐ Red Cat
Witterly Woods
☎ 01257 263 966
Last orders: 2.00pm and 10.00pm.
11.00pm on Sundays.
££

There has been an inn here since 1805 and is now a cheerful Italian place obviously specialising in Italian food served in the flagstoned eating areas. There is a playground and a beer garden where dogs are encouraged. It has recently changed hands.

M62

Liverpool to Hull

1 to **38**

One of the few motorways which runs laterally across the country. It is 108 miles long and was completed in 1976 to link the ports of Liverpool and Hull. It does not lend itself to gastronomic feasts.

WESTERN SECTION

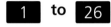

1 to **26**

With the best will in the world this part, from Liverpool to beyond Manchester, is not pretty. However once past Junction 21 it climbs up into the Pennines and Junction 22 could be a remote spot for picnics near the top, but marred by endless lamp posts on the motorway. It then descends into the industrial area by Huddersfield and Bradford.

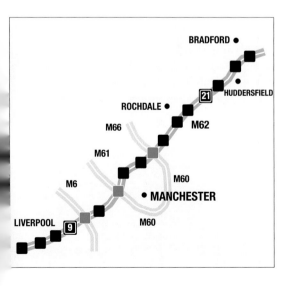

9 Newton Warrington A49

Head for the Church. The Swan is on the road forking to the right.

Ⓐ The Swan

Winwick

☎ 01925 631 416

Last orders: 10.00pm. 9.30pm on Sundays.

££ 🛏

The present building dates from 1898 and is an offshoot of the Chef and Brewer. There are 42 double bedrooms in a modern extension, with a restaurant and a bar in the older part. It also caters for conferences. Some outside seating where dogs are permitted. A comfort stop.

21 Milnrow
Shaw A640

Not as difficult as it looks, but the road through this ex mining town needs concentration.

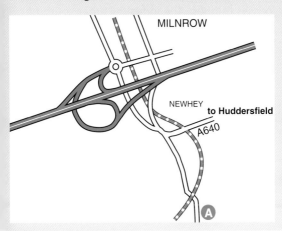

Ⓐ **The Jubilee**
Shaw
☎ 01706 847 540
Last orders: 2.00pm. No meals on Saturdays.
££

So named after the Jubilee Colliery which is down the road but now closed. It is open for lunches only and closed on Saturdays. Privately owned it gives a friendly welcome to visitors. It specialises in Leg of Lamb served in the restaurant cum bar. Outside seating where dogs are welcome.

EASTERN SECTION

27 to **38**

Not the most attractive part of England as it passes through the industrial areas south of Leeds. However once past the intersection with the A1(M) and the famous Ferrybridge Power Station, the surroundings become more rural, excepting the odd slag heap or power station. It is flat and level full of drainage ditches and fens. The M62 crosses over the Humber at Goole with views over the surrounding countryside. The tower of the Minster at Howden is impressive and the inland port of Goole is to the south made visible by the cranes. The motorway ceases just short of Brough, an old Roman town which was the ferry point for those crossing over the Humber in those days. It continues as a dual carriageway to Hull and the present day ferry port for Rotterdam.

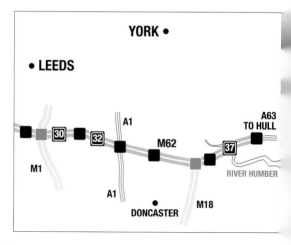

30 Rothwell
Wakefield A642

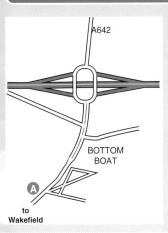

A642

BOTTOM
BOAT

A

to
Wakefield

Easy enough to
find the Spindle
Tree.

Spindle Tree
Stanley
☎ 01924 824 810
Last orders: 2.00pm and 9.00pm
No evening meals on Sundays.
££

A small wayside pub now owned by Pub
Masters who have recently bought it. They
have refurbished it with open areas for eating
and a bar. It has a cheerful and friendly
atmosphere. Outside seating in a garden at the
rear.

32   Pontefract   Castleford A639

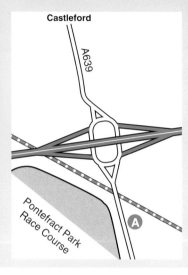

Castleford

A639

Pontefract
Race Course

Ⓐ

Handy for those
going to the
Races.

Places of interest
Pontefract
Racecourse.

Ⓐ Parkside Hotel
Pontefract
☎ 01977 709 911
Last orders: 2.30pm and 9.30pm.
9.00pm on Sundays.
££ 🛏

A privately owned hotel with 29 bedrooms, a
restaurant and a Long Bar where bar meals are
served. A playground, beer garden, outside
seating and a large carpark, overlooked by
what was one of the last remaining working
coal mines. A comfort stop.

37 Howden A614 Selby A63

Howden was once famous for one of Europe's largest horse fairs. Until some twenty years ago it had degenerated into a one-horse town. It is now a thriving picturesque place.

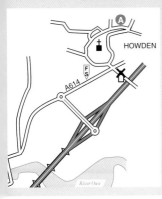

Places of interest
Howden Minster.
The former
Summer Palace
of the Bishops of
Durham.

Ⓐ

Wellington Hotel
Howden
☎ 01430 430 258
Last orders: 2.00pm and 9.30pm.
££

Once a coaching inn it still gives board and lodging to the passing motorist. It has 10 bedrooms, a restaurant and bars with piped music. At the rear is a beer garden.
A comfort stop.

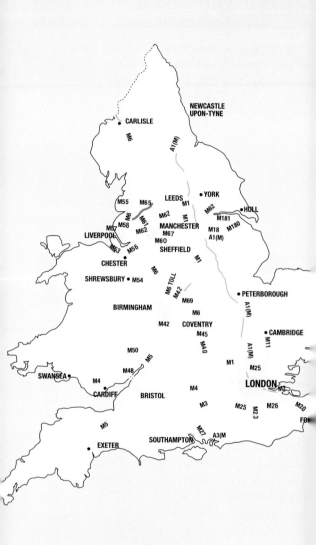

M65

Preston to Colne

1 to **14**

For many years the M65 was a short isolated stretch from Blackburn to Colne. It has now been continued to link with the M6 at Preston.

There is not much to say about it except that you are driving through the last remaining vestiges of the Lancashire cotton industry with huge palatials factories of Italianate architecture. The plus side is the comforting bulk of the Pennines which is visible on both sides of the motorway..

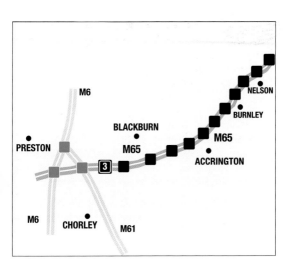

3   Blackburn   Chorley A674   Bolton A675

The roundabout at the end of the lead off could be confusing.

Places of interest
Hoghton Tower. (HHA)

Ⓐ # Hoghton Arms
Withnell
☎ 01254 201 083
Last orders: 9.00pm. 8.30pm on Sundays.
££

The building has been there since 1704, and has been a pub long before 1910. It has recently been greatly extended to provide more eating areas with a restaurant and bar. Fires but of the gas log variety. Outside a playground and seating.
Dogs are not
encouraged.
A comfort
stop.

3 Blackburn Chorley A674
Bolton A675

B ## The Boatyard Inn
Riley Green
☎ 01254 209 841
Last orders: 9.30pm. 9pm on Fridays.
££

Once a boat yard by the Leeds and Liverpool
Canal, it has now been converted by
Thwaites Brewery into a waterside inn with
large open areas. Dogs allowed outdoors
but children not encouraged,
for obvious
reasons.

C ## Ristorante Alghergo
Withnell
☎ 01254 202 222
Last orders: 10.30pm (Evenings only)
On Sundays from 12.00am to 10.00pm.
£££

As the name implies this is an Italian
restaurant which has a good local
reputation and a friendly atmosphere.

M69

Coventry to Leicester

M69

1 to **2**

This motorway was built in the mid 1970s to give direct access between Coventry and Leicester. It is comparatively little used so is useful to those who are using the M1 and M40 as a means of driving north or south. The junction with the M1 is rather abrupt as a result of a decision at the time not to make it into a proper clover leaf as the volume of traffic would not warrant the expense. The building of the motorways has had the curious effect of isolating corners of the countryside to create rural areas of calm, such as the part around Bosworth Field ("-my Kingdom for a horse").

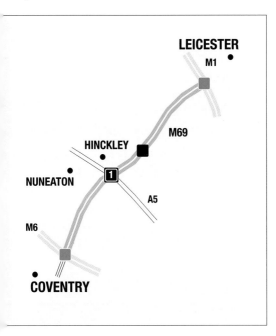

1   Nuneaton   Lutterworth A5

This junction intersects with the A5 (the Roman Watling Street) which until the building of the M1 and the M6 was the main road to Birmingham.

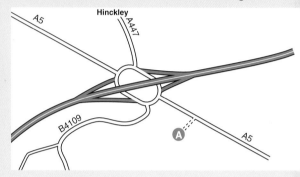

Places of interest
Bosworth Field. 1485.

Barnacles Restaurant
Nr Hinckley
☎ 01455 633 220
Last orders: 2.00pm and 9.00pm.
Lunch only onSaturdays.Closed Sundays.
£££

A privately owned restaurant in pleasant grounds with a lake. It specialises in fish food and there is a separately owned shop next to the restaurant which sells fish. Dogs are not welcomed and there are no special facilities for children.

Journey From to

1 to 5

A short 27 mile stretch from the M18 towards Grimsby, the last 15 miles being dual carriageway. It begins at the intersection with the M18, then crosses flat fenlands which were drained by the Dutch, before passing the much maligned steelworks town of Scunthorpe. It goes through pleasant wooded expanses of countryside to Junction 5. From there it continues as a dual carriageway to Grimsby and the link road to the Humber Bridge and Hull leads off to the left. The Whistle and Flute in Barnetby le Wold will give you lunch and dinner..

There are some interesting places to see in the neighbourhood, such as the Saxon church at Barton on Humber, the imposing intact brick gatehouse of Thornton Abbey and the old market town of Brigg.

Those with a knowledge of Roman history will know that at Junction 4 the motorway crosses Ermine Street from Lincoln to the crossing point over the Humber to Brough.

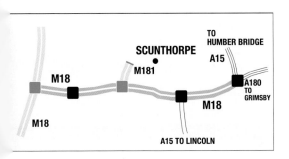

ABERDEEN

DUNDEE

PERTH

M90

M9
•STIRLING
M80
M9
M73 M876 M8
M8 M77
GLASGOW

EDINBURGH

M74

A74(M)

THE MOTORWAY NETWORK

Scotland

Motorway introduction

Scotland may extend a warm welcome to visitors and even Sassenachs, but for the motorway user you get the impression that the Scots have forgotten the art of hospitality to the passing traveller. Part of this impression may be due to the fact that the new motorways, except for the M74, do not follow the old coaching routes, but the same can be said for England. There are some excellent exceptions to the rule but there were a lot which did not come up to scratch. On the M8 for example, from Edinburgh to Glasgow, there is not one single place worthy of being mentioned.

The most tedious aspect of the Scottish motorways is the system of linked junctions. It might save money but it generates unnecessary driving on minor roads.

ABERDEEN

DUNDEE

PERTH•

M90

M9

•STIRLING

M80

M9

M73 M876 M8

M8 M77

EDINBURGH

GLASGOW

M74

A74(M)

M9

Edinburgh to Stirling

1 to **11**

Starting near the Airport it passes through agricultural country and old shale heaps.

You then drive past the impressive ruins of Linlithgow Palace, once one of the great buildings of Europe, admired by the French princesses who were married to Scottish kings. It was burnt in 1745 during the Jacobite Rebellion and has been roofless ever since, but there are rumours that parts could be re-roofed.

The motorway ends north of the equally impressive Stirling Castle, the favourite refuge for the Scottish kings, which was remodelled by James V and is a fine example of Rennaisance architecture.

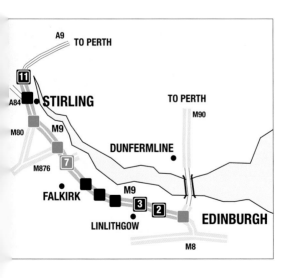

2. Forth Rd Bridge (A904)
3. Linlithgow A803   Bo'ness

Like most of the junctions these are linked
together, depending upon the direction of travel.
Apart from the one mentioned below, there are
other places in Linlithgow to suit most
requirements.

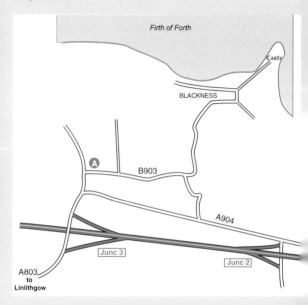

Places of interest
Hopetoun House (HHA).
The House of The Binns (NTS) .
Blackness Castle(HS).
Linlithgow Palace(HS).

2&3 2. Forth Rd Bridge (A904)
3. Linlithgow A803   Bo'ness

 A

Champany Inn
Champany
☎ 01506 834 532
Last orders: 2.00pm and 10.00pm.
The main restaurant is not open on Sundays
nor Saturday Lunch.
££££   🛏   *

It is one of the best known restaurants in
Scotland. It was once a farm house where
Mary Queen of Scots used to come over from
Linlithgow to have picnics, hence the name.
The Inn also has 16 bedrooms should you not
be tempted to drive on again after dinner.
There is outside seating for hot days and a
Bistro to suit the more hurried motorist. It is
noted for Aberdeen Angus beef and has been
named as Meat Restaurant of Great Britain as
well as Best Restaurant of the Year.

7   Kincardine   Stirling   A905

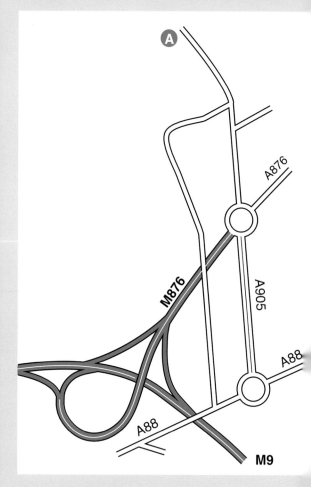

Places of interest
The Pineapple, Dunmore Park (NTS).

Airth Castle and Hotel.
Airth.
☎ 01324 831 411
Last orders: 2.00pm and 9.45pm.
£££ 🛏

It was once the castle home, since the 14th century, of the Barons of Airth and Lords of Elphinstone. It is now a 3 Star hotel owned by Radisson SAS.

The castle itself has 23 bedrooms and a restaurant, whilst over at the former stables, now fully converted, there are a further 99 bedrooms and another restaurant together with a cocktail bar.

Part of the grounds have been developed with modern housing but the gardens surrounding the castle and the view over towards Falkirk are good. The disabled are catered for. Children and dogs are welcome.

11 Doune B824 Dunblane B8033 Bridge of Allan A9

After coming off the roundabout, drive towards the outskirts of the Bridge of Allan. Just before the said bridge, with a high wooded bluff on the other side of the river, turn right. The Inn is to the right.

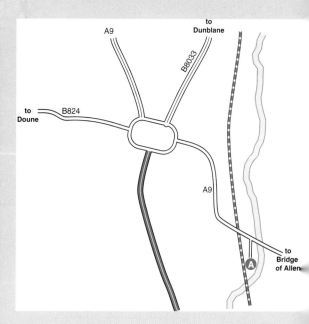

Places of interest
Doune Castle.
Stirling Castle(HS).
Argyll's Lodging (HS).
The Wallace Monument.

Doune B824 Dunblane B8033
Bridge of Allan A9

The Old Bridge Inn
Bridge of Allan
☎ 01786 833 335
Last orders: 2.30pm and 8.45pm.
£££

The Inn was built in 1710 by the bridge which was first constructed in 1520 and rebuilt in 1695. It was originally surrounded by mills and by Willie's brewery famous for making good beer. The interior has been stripped out to make a larger area with rough stone walls and timber panelling. There is an uncommonly fine foliated stone mantlepiece which must have arrived from elsewhere. The owner collects old typewriters and home cine projectors. A bell from the Temple Church in Glasgow will let customers know when they have overstayed their welcome.

M74/A74(M)

Glasgow to Carlisle

4 to **24**

Within the last few years the A74 has been rebuilt to motorway standards. North of junction 13 it is the M74, and south to the Border it is the A74(M). It is the most scenic motorway in Scotland as between junctions 12 and 16 it passes through the Southern Uplands and the head waters of the river Clyde.
There seems to be a reluctance to join up with the M6 to make it a continuous motorway but perhaps there is a hidden agenda to keep the system independent and uncontaminated by the English roads and numbering.

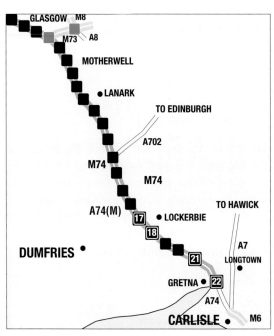

17	Lockerbie B7078 Dumfries (A709)

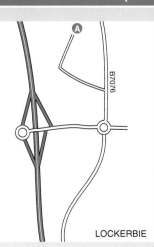

B7076

LOCKERBIE

An easy junction. You can see the hotel as soon as you get off the motorway.

Places of interest
Lochmaben Castle (HS)
Rammerscales (HHA).

Ⓐ Dryfesdale Hotel

Nr Lockerbie
☎ 01576 202 427
Last orders: 2.00pm and 9.00pm.
££ 🛏 Breakfast ✳

The house was built in the late 17th century as the Manse, but was converted into a hotel in the early 1900s. It is now a family run hotel with 16 bedrooms, a restaurant and a bar catering for lunches and dinners. Dogs are welcomed. Facilities for the disabled. Breakfast for the passing motorist from 7am.

17&18 Lockerbie B723
Dumfries (A709)

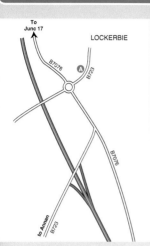

Another restricted junction, so for those driving north you have to rejoin at Junction 17and vice versa.

Ⓐ Somerton House Hotel and Resturant

Lockerbie

☎ 01576 202 583

Last orders: 2.00pm and 9.00pm every day

££ 🍴 Breakfast until 9.00am.

A privately owned hotel with a friendly atmosphere. It has 11 well furnished bedrooms, a restaurant, conservatory and bars as well as a car park and garden. Dogs and children welcome.

21&22 Annan
Canonbie B6357

Not easy to follow, but at least you can get on and off from both directions.

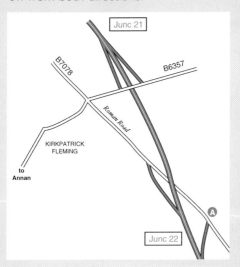

A ## The Mill
Grahamshill
☎ 01461 800 344
Last orders: 8.45pm. Dinners only.
£users

The Mill started life as a farmhouse in 1740 and was converted into a hotel and restaurant in the 1990s. It has 27 bedrooms and a restaurant and a bar, all on one level so it is disabled friendly. Children and dogs are welcome.

Glasgow to Carlisle

25 Longton A6071
Gretna Green B7076

This is really for those coming from the south
and even then it is a marathon getting back
onto the motorway. Those driving down from
the north deserve a medal for map-reading to
reach the hotel.

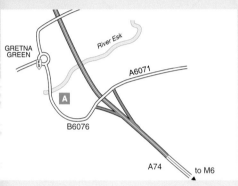

A ## The Gretna Chase Hotel
Gretna Green
☎ 01461 337 517
Last orders: 3.00pm and 9.30pm.
£££

It was built in 1865 by the owner of the Toll
Bar over the river to house runaway couples
who had to spend a statutory two weeks in
residence before being allowed to wed. It is
still a family run hotel with 9
bedrooms and a comfortable
restaurant and bar.
Dogs allowed
but outdoors.

ABERDEEN

DUNDEE

PERTH

M90

M9

STIRLING

M80   M9

M73 M876 M8

M8   M77

GLASGOW

EDINBURGH

M74

A74(M)

M90

Edinburgh to Perth

■1■ to ■10■

An interesting motorway as you pass Loch Leven, where Mary Queen of Scots was imprisoned, to the right with the Lomond Hills beyond. Further on the motorway climbs gently up to Glenfarg and then drops down to cross the Bridge of Earn. Beyond Moncrieffe Hill are the outskirts of Perth and to the north can be seen the looming mass of the the Highlands.

There are castles such as Huntingtower and Elcho to be seen and to the east is Abernethy where William the Conqueror took the personal submission of the Scottish king Malcolm Canmore in 1072.

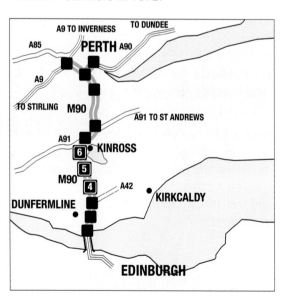

| **4** | Kelty A909
 Dollar B914 |

You can see the Butterchurn from the motorway when coming from the south.

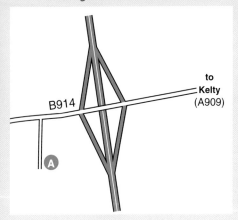

A **The Butterchurn,**
Kelty.
☎ 01383 830 169.
Last orders; From 9.00am to 9.00pm.
High Teas between 4.30pm and 6.00pm.
£££

Once a farm, which then started a sideline in teas and coffees. It has now joined the modern world with a major rebuilding scheme creating a comfortable restaurant and a gift and crafts shop. Farm animals roam around, so no dogs.

5 Crook of Devon B9097
     Glenrothes

The hotel which is about two miles away, seems further than you would expect.

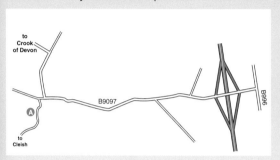

(A) # Nivingston House Hotel,
Cleish
☎ 01577 850 216
Last orders: 2.00pm and 9.00pm.
£££ 🛏 Breakfast ∗

A family owned hotel set in 12 acres of garden at the foot of the Cleish Hills. The Victorian addition masks the original building of 1725. It has 9 bedrooms with a restaurant, bar and a lounge. Morning coffee and teas. Children and dogs permitted. Breakfasts for passing motorists, but give warning.

269

6   Kinross A977

The private road to the Grouse and Claret is opposite the Esso Filling Station. If it is full, there are at least four good hotels in Kinross.

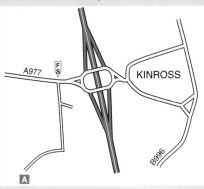

Places of Interest: Loch Leven Castle.(HS)
Kinross House Garden (HHA)

A   The Grouse and Claret,
Heatheryford.
☎ 01577 864 212.
Last orders; From 2.30pm to 7.00pm.
Closed on Sundays in Winter.
£££

A surprisingly peaceful spot, with a large garden looking onto a small loch. An imaginative menu, with a hint of the East, (but specialising in venison, salmon; fish and cheese souffles) in a comfortable restaurant with a bar. For the famished in mind, there is an art gallery.

Notes

Notes

Alphabetical Index

Alphabetical Index

Alphabetical Index

Alphabetical Index

Alphabetical Index

Alphabetical Index

Alphabetical Index

Name	Motorway	Exit	Page
Wheatsheaf	M4	23a	89
Wheatsheaf	M6	11	123
White Hart	A1(M)	6	2
White Hart	A1(M)	13/14	7
White Hart	M2	2	56
White Hart	M25	6	179
White Hart	M27	1	189
White Horse	M11	12	155
White Swan	A1(M)	34	11
White Swan	M1	47	53
Windmill	M6	19	128
Windmill	M20	8	170
Wooden Walls of Old England			
	M1	15	41
Wye Knot	M48	2	204
Yanwath Gate Inn	M6	40	140
Yellow Lion	M1	31	50

SCOTLAND

Name	Motorway	Exit	Page
Airth Castle & Hotel	M9	7	257
Butterchurn	M90	4	268
Champany Inn	M9	2/3	255
Dryfesdale Hotel	A74(M)	17	262
Gretna Chase Hotel	A74(M)	25	265
Grouse & Claret	M90	6	270
Mill	A74(M)	21/22	264
Livingston House Hotel	M90	5	269
Old Bridge Inn	M9	11	259
Somerton House Hotel	A74(M)	17/18	263

Index by Motorways

ENGLAND & WALES

Index by Motorways

Index by Motorways

Index by Motorways

Index by Motorways

Index by Motorways

SCOTLAND

M9

M74/A74(M)

M90

READERS' RESPONSE

If you think that we have missed any places which should be included or that circumstances have altered, such as a change of ownership, which would mean an addition, amendment or even deletion, then please let us know using the following page(s).

If your suggestions are included in the next issue, we will send you a free copy of the new edition.

Name . . . .
Address . . . .
. . . .
Post Code . . . . .TN . . . .
I would suggest that "A Break Off the Motorways" be amended as follows:

Inclusions
Name . . . .
Motorway . . . . .Junction . . . .Location . . . .
Details . . . .
. . . .
. . . .

Amendments
Name. . . . .
Motorway . . . . .Junction . . . .Location . . . .
Details . . . .
. . . .
. . . .

Deletions
Name . . . .
Motorway . . . . .Junction . . . . .Location . . . .
Details . . . .
. . . .
. . . .

READERS' RESPONSE

If you think that we have missed any places which should be included or that circumstances have altered, such as a change of ownership, which would mean an addition, amendment or even deletion, then please let us know using the following page(s).

If your suggestions are included in the next issue, we will send you a free copy of the new edition.

Name . . . .

Address . . . .

. . . .

Post Code . . . . .TN . . . .

I would suggest that "A Break Off the Motorways" be amended as follows:

Inclusions

Name . . . .

Motorway . . . . .Junction . . . .Location . . . .

Details . . . .

. . . .

. . . .

Amendments

Name. . . . .

Motorway . . . . .Junction . . . .Location . . . .

Details . . . .

. . . .

. . . .

Deletions

Name . . . .

Motorway . . . . .Junction . . . . .Location . . . .

Details . . . .

. . . .

. . . .

READERS' RESPONSE

If you think that we have missed any places which should be included or that circumstances have altered, such as a change of ownership, which would mean an addition, amendment or even deletion, then please let us know using the following page(s).

If your suggestions are included in the next issue, we will send you a free copy of the new edition.

Name . . . .
Address . . . .
. . . .
Post Code . . . . .TN . . . .
I would suggest that "A Break Off the Motorways" be amended as follows:

Inclusions
Name . . . .
Motorway . . . . .Junction . . . .Location . . . .
Details . . . .
. . . .
. . . .

Amendments
Name. . . . .
Motorway . . . . .Junction . . . .Location . . . .
Details . . . .
. . . .
. . . .

Deletions
Name . . . .
Motorway . . . . .Junction . . . . .Location . . . .
Details . . . .
. . . .
. . . .

Reader's Purchase Order Form

In the event that you are unable to easily obtain a copy of "A Break from the Motorways" from your local bookshop and would like to purchase one direct from the publishers, please complete the details below.

Please send me .... copy/s of A Break from the Motorways.

I enclose a cheque for £............ being the cost of the guide at £9.95 plus £1.00 postage and packing per copy.

Name: ....

Address: ....

....

....

Post Code: .... ☎: ....

Special Instructions:

....

....

....